WORKING FIRE IN EAST CLEVELAND

ACTION, HARD-HITTING HUMOR, & RAW HONESTY TELL THE STORY OF INNER-CITY CAREER FIREFIGHTER

MICHAEL C. EDE

Fire Photo: Chad Johns | Cleveland Skyline: by DJ Johnson on Unsplash
Cover Design: Daniel Rg Crandall

PIXEL GLYPH PRESS

PIXELGLYPHPRESS.COM

June, 1998, Mike Ede in new truck 121
credit: Jerry Kirchner

WORKING FIRE IN EAST CLEVELAND

by

Michael C. Ede

WORKING FIRE IN EAST CLEVELAND

Action, hard-hitting humor, & raw honesty
tell the story of inner-city career Firefighter

Michael C. Ede

Description: A career firefighter with a personal commitment that "everyone gets home safe," shares true stories of emergency calls, working relationships, and life inside and outside of the firehouse in the financially and morally crumbling city of East Cleveland, Ohio.

© Copyright 2025 Michael C. Ede,
All rights reserved. Any use, reproduction, or storage of this content or derivative works in any format is strictly prohibited without written permission from the author/and or publisher.

Contains adult language and situations.
Recommended for readers 18+

This story contains actual events and real people in high-stress and dangerous situations. The stories in this book are honest recollections and interpretations of events by the author. Narrative, emphasis, selective story telling, and opinions have been included to create a more engaging, humorous, or impactful retelling of these real-life events. Some names and details have been changed to protect the private rights of individuals. Every effort has been made to supply complete and accurate information. Daniel Rg Crandall Publisher assumes no responsibility or liability for inaccuracies, the identity of persons or places or any infringement or other rights of third parties, which may result from the descriptions and characterizations provided by the author.

Paperback
ISBN: 978-1-956579-88-8

Adult Non-fiction, biography, memoir

Pixel Glyph Press
an imprint of Daniel Rg Crandall Publisher
PIXELGLYPHPRESS.COM

Contents

	Foreword	6
CHAPTER 1	War Story 1: *Trapped*	9
CHAPTER 2	Old School	17
CHAPTER 3	The Brotherhood	20
CHAPTER 4	So, You Want to Be a Firefighter	24
CHAPTER 5	First Day in the Hood	27
CHAPTER 6	Fire School	33
CHAPTER 7	In House	37
CHAPTER 8	War Stories – Introducing Charlie Catania	43
CHAPTER 9	War Story 2: *Lakefront Fire*	45
CHAPTER 10	Black & White	52
CHAPTER 11	War Story 3: *Elevator Fatality*	62
CHAPTER 12	Ball Busting	67
CHAPTER 13	Real Heroes… or Not?	73
CHAPTER 14	Perimeter Man	80
CHAPTER 15	War Story 4: *The Ultimate Paradise*	84
CHAPTER 16	Squad Knobs	88
CHAPTER 17	Fire Boss	98
CHAPTER 18	War Story 5: *Sudden Death*	109
CHAPTER 19	Nine Dead in Charleston, South Carolina	115
CHAPTER 20	Bizarre Events & Outrageous Behavior	125
CHAPTER 21	The Edge	136
CHAPTER 22	War Story 6: *Triple-header*	141
CHAPTER 23	Fire Chief	153
CHAPTER 24	Rumors	158
CHAPTER 25	Promotions	171
CHAPTER 26	Circling the Drain	178
CHAPTER 27	The Blowout	185

Foreword

    This book is about life in the fire service with a busy urban fire department located in East Cleveland, Ohio. It is an appraisal of actual emergencies, as well as life inside of the engine house, spanning a 26-year career.

    I've tried to be as factual as possible without embarrassing, humiliating, or defaming any people involved. Some names were changed to protect the innocent, as well as the guilty. Nothing was sugar-coated or fabricated. Some of the stories are gut-wrenching. Others are hilarious. Still others are action-packed. But the one thing they all have in common is that they are true. The book runs the entire gamut of emotions and portrays, as nearly as possible, the life of a firefighter both in and out of the engine house, without too much drama or a love story attached.

    This book is dedicated to all active and retired East Cleveland firefighters. I have the utmost respect and admiration for these brave individuals and the reputation they have achieved over the years as hard-charging interior firefighters. A special dedication goes out to the late Captain Charlie Catania, my friend and mentor. Loved by many, he went too soon. It is also dedicated to all of the firefighters who died on 9-11-01 at the World Trade Center Towers in New York City, and to every fallen firefighter all over the world, as well as their families. Special thanks go out to all men and women who are, or were, a part of the United States military. I will always respect and appreciate them for their ultimate sacrifice of fighting for the freedom we all enjoy in this great country.

I would like to thank God for giving me this opportunity to enjoy a great life with my family. I want to thank my wife Lynn for always being there for me and for being a fantastic mother to our two children. To my son Michael and daughter Shannon, thank you for being good, respectful, and fun-loving children. You are my world, my best friends and I'm extremely proud of both of you.

I would like to thank my role model and mother, the late Ruth C. Ede, for being the toughest, most giving, and nicest person I've ever met. She raised nine children by herself and did a phenomenal job. Special thanks go out to my mother-in-law, the late Barbara Priesse. Barb helped us in so many ways, especially with raising our children in their very young years. I will never forget her. Rest in peace, sweet "Buttercup."

I would also like to thank my six awesome brothers, Tony, Terry, Tim, Tom, Ted, and Dan, as well as my two sisters, Ellen and Janet, who are two of the most genuine, kind, and helpful ladies I've ever known. The good Lord truly blessed me with the family I have.

I hope that you all enjoy reading this book as much as I did writing it. God Bless!

Dispatcher: "9-1-1, what's your emergency??"

9-1-1 caller: "I smoked some crystal meth and passed out. When I woke up, my ass hurt. So I took a shower and found my asshole was crusty! I think my roommate's dog raped me!" (Actual 9-1-1 call)

CHAPTER 1

War Story 1: *Trapped*

I had just poured my second cup of coffee after our short morning meeting. It seemed like my shift was catching most of the fires this year, so it was no surprise when the station 2 direct phone line rang shortly after 9 A.M. with a report of a fire in an apartment building on Taylor Road.

I was the officer in charge of Ladder Truck 121 that day and we would be the first arriving truck on scene. Upon our arrival, I saw light smoke escaping from the left side of the building out of a third-floor window. Something was burning, but it did not appear to be very serious.

After investigating the apartment, we discovered that a mattress had caught fire from careless smoking and was smoldering considerably. These types of fires are nuisances because you have to tear apart the mattress and extinguish all burning embers, and there is no excitement in doing so. We emptied out a couple of pressurized water fire extinguishers onto the mattress, rolled it up and tossed it out the window. We set up a large smoke ejector to ventilate the smoke from the suite. We were probably on scene for 45 minutes, then returned to quarters.

I put my cold cup of coffee into the microwave and just as I closed the door, the hot line rang again. This call came in as "a working house fire with children trapped." It's not often that you get this call, but when you do, the pace and the adrenalin flow increase dramatically. Everyone moves faster, dreading the thought of pulling young, burned children out of smoke and flames.

The fire was in a two-family house on the corner of East 133rd Street and Milan Avenue. We were responding one firefighter short because the ambulance was out of quarters when the call came in. Our normal procedure for a fire run was to have a firefighter from the ambulance jump over to the truck to make it a four-man crew. Today we'd pick up another firefighter at the scene. The fourth man makes a big difference; it gives you a man to stretch out the hose line outside to assure that there are no kinks and then work inside with the other two members of the attack crew. The driver makes up the fourth crew member.

We responded down Shaw Avenue. I focused on keeping myself calm in order to think clearly and make good decisions when we arrived on scene. As we approached Milan Avenue, I could see thick, dark smoke billowing from the corner house's second-floor window. On the sidewalk, a citizen was squirting water from a garden hose into the window. "At least I know where the fire is," I said to driver/operator Trammel Tucker as we slowed to a stop.

Tucker positioned truck 121 directly in front of the structure, just as he was supposed to do. Firefighter Dennis Dixon grabbed a pre-connected hose line and we made our way toward the side door. A resident waved and told us that we needed to enter from the front. This little bit of information proved crucial. It was a two-family home, and had we entered the wrong door, we would have wasted precious time. I have learned over the years that a short interview of residents can be invaluable in the quest to finding interior stairwells and access points to upper floors.

As we made our way toward the Milan Avenue front door, I approached our officer in charge (O.I.C.) and asked him if everyone had gotten out of the house. He said that it was reported that everyone had. This was reassuring, but I knew not to take this kind of information as fact. I proceeded, cautiously optimistic that the kids had gotten out safely.

The front door was wide open. Firefighter Dennis Dixon and I took a knee on the porch and put on our breathing apparatus masks. Firefighter Jeff Polk was assigned to be the third member of our attack crew, and he also masked up on the front porch. We would be taking the first hose line into the structure.

I felt certain that the fire was on the second floor because of the smoke we saw coming from the window and the citizen futilely attempting to extinguish the fire with the garden hose. I looked in through the front door and saw the stairs leading to the second floor just off to our right. It would be a no brainer to get to this fire, I thought.

There was a hell of a lot of smoke on the first floor but no visible flame in the living room. This was a red flag that I later realized I should have paid more attention to. I radioed truck 121 to charge the hose line and after the water filled the hose, we proceeded up the stairs to the second floor with Firefighter Dixon on the nozzle, followed by myself, then Firefighter Polk shagging hose. This was going to be a "textbook knock" on this very hot, raging fire.

We made our way through the thick smoke to the second floor through zero visibility and all the way to the bedroom where we had seen the smoke coming from earlier. But there was no orange glow indicating the presence of fire. We could feel the heat all around, but we saw no flame.

We found and opened two other bedroom doors but still, no flames.

We had been on the second floor now for about three minutes, crawling low on the floor, looking for this fire, with a gradual increase in heat. The heat suddenly increased dramatically, and I knew it was time to get the hell out. "Back out now!" I yelled. "We gotta get out right now!"

Polk and I did belly slides down the top stairs to the landing area. Dixon was nearby on the nozzle and would soon follow us down. As we rushed to escape the unbearable heat, it suddenly became even hotter. My helmet got knocked off my head and as I turned to put it back on, I saw a massive orange fireball only a few feet from where we were on the landing. The fire was on its way up the stairs and we were backing down directly into it. Never had I experienced that much heat at such a close range. It was like being thrown directly into the gates of hell.

It was clear now that the fire had started on the first floor and was making its way up the stairs directly on top of our hose line, threatening to burn through it and render it useless. At that moment I thought that we could die or at least suffer serious burns. We did a very swift about-face and retreated, this time back up the stairs toward the bedroom.

"I'm burning up!" yelled Polk. He was still new at the time, with less than two years in the department. I was impressed that he wasn't freaking out. I yelled back that I was burning up too, and he told me later that hearing that helped him keep his composure.

I called out to Dixon to try to find the bedroom window as a secondary means of escape. Dixon was an ex-U.S. Army Ranger who had participated in the covert rescue mission in Somalia depicted in the movie Blackhawk Down. Dixon quickly found the window and called out to us. The only thought in my mind was escaping the heat. I knew there was an excellent chance that our attack hose line on the stairway would soon burst from the flames.

I radioed the O.I.C. and called for a ground ladder to the second-floor window for our escape. I knew that the O.I.C. and others with radios outside would pick up on the sense of urgency in my voice. But my portable radio failed and my transmission was not heard. Hearing my call and the silence that followed, Dixon leaned out the window and banged on the vinyl siding in an attempt to get somebody's attention. His efforts were also in vain. I called for the nozzle as we all hunkered down low to the ground in the bedroom, prepared to bail out the window without a ladder if the hose line burst and the heat became unbearable.

I opened the nozzle and started knocking down the fire that was quickly approaching us from below. Polk was behind me. I called out to Dixon to get ready to bail out. True to his Army Ranger roots, he said something that I will never forget: "Not without y'all! We go out together!"

We crouched down flat on our bellies in an effort to stay under the heat. I continued to apply water from our hose onto the fire without any rupture. Shortly after I opened the nozzle on the fire, a crew on the first floor also began to attack the fire from their location below. We were all near enough the window to bail out now and I was fairly confident that if we did, we may get hurt, but would most likely survive the jump of about fifteen feet. Regardless, jumping would have to be our last resort.

In a little more than a minute's time, the heat seemed to stabilize, then began to diminish. This was comforting, but we knew that we were far from out of the woods yet. We continued to flow water and ventilate smoke from the second-floor window until our low-air alarms sounded on our breathing apparatus. By this time the main body of the fire was extinguished and we would soon be in the overhaul stage of this fire.

Together, our three-man crew proceeded down the previously fire-engulfed stairway, to the first floor, and out the front door. It was a beautiful sight to see daylight again. At this point I realized that my strength was completely sapped. The adrenalin rush was now replaced by heat exhaustion. We walked to the front yard and collapsed on the grass. I knew that we just escaped serious injury or possible death. The feeling was overwhelming and all I could do was lie there. My entire body was drenched with sweat and my face felt sunburned.

Paramedics asked me if I was okay, and I just nodded that I was, without speaking. Nobody outside had a clue as to what we had just gone through.

Finally, I was able to sit up and drink some water. I can't remember ever being so thirsty. Tucker poured water on my neck in an effort to lower my body temperature. I probably should have gone to the hospital for heat exhaustion, but my stubborn Irish pride got in the way. Although firefighting operations were still under way, I was out of commission for about twenty minutes.

When I finally gained some strength, I went back inside to be with the crews that were inside extinguishing the smoldering embers, looking for hidden fire and hot spots. But Polk, Dixon and I were still physically beat. We were going through the motions, but the harrowing situation that we just experienced still weighed heavily on our minds. Polk was eventually taken to the hospital for treatment. He had sustained second-degree burns to his ears and wrists. Dixon received the same superficial burns on his face that I did.

When the smoke cleared, we were able to examine the hose for physical damage. A two-foot section of the outer jacket of the hose was burned off and hanging loosely like shedding skin from a snake. It was amazing that this line stayed intact. I thanked God for keeping my crew safe.

When we returned to quarters I showered and ate lunch, and felt much better. Exhaustion was eventually replaced by anger. The failure of my portable radio was unacceptable. Problems with our radios had been an ongoing issue. That, and the fact that many of our firefighters were wearing hand-me-down, sub-standard gear, also bothered me more than usual. Polk may not have sustained second-degree burns had he been given new turnout gear when he was hired.

I dashed off a letter to the Fire Chief complaining of these two things. As usual, the story from the Fire Chief's office was that there was no money to upgrade the equipment. Unfortunately, this was true. In East Cleveland, we get a lot of tough fires and we wear out our firefighting turnout gear and radios faster than the average fire department.

But this fire turned out to be a tremendous training tool for our department. In our review of the incident, we noted that things aren't always as they appear to be. For example, we gave too much emphasis to the citizen with the garden hose. We had assumed that the fire was in the second-floor bedroom because that's where the smoke was coming from. The other first and second floor windows were intact. Later we determined that it was in the first-floor kitchen. I should have found the fire and directed the first hose line into the kitchen. That was the first mistake and I owned it. The second mistake was that the second-in crew took too long getting their hose line in place to protect our stairwell. We had our initial line charged with water and up the stairs in about one minute. It took the second line over four minutes to get charged. This was way too long. But we swallowed our pride and openly discussed these mistakes in order to avoid making them again.

The effects of this emergency lingered with me. Physically, I didn't feel right for weeks. I went to the doctor to have my heart checked out. After thorough testing, I was given a clean bill of health. I don't know exactly what happened, but the intense heat took a toll on my 53-year-old body, more than any in my career. It took about five to six weeks before I really felt like I was back to normal.

I responded to many fires in my career and most of them run together in my mind. This fire was one that the three of us will never forget because we knew that we flirted with serious injury and cheated death that day. If that hose line had burst it could have been so much worse!

9-1-1 caller: "Can y'all come get this skunk out my basement?"

Dispatcher: "Only if the skunk is on fire, ma'am!"

(Actual 9-1-1 call)

CHAPTER 2

Old School

One of the first things that you learn in the fire service is that the traditions, policies, and procedures that are in place in today's fire departments were shaped and initiated by brave, dedicated men and women. This tradition-rich occupation got its start in the 1800s and has evolved considerably due to advances in technology. But many of the principles that were started back in those days still remain in place today. I will always be grateful to those firefighters who came before us and for their contributions to this honorable profession.

It's mind-boggling to me that old-school firefighters entered burning buildings without the aid of a self-contained breathing apparatus (SCBA). The first primitive breathing apparatuses for firefighting were developed in the 1920s and '30s, and were not mandatory until 1982. In the East Cleveland Fire Department during the 1970's, firefighters were forbidden to wear a breathing apparatus unless instructed by an officer. I started my career in 1988, and even then, many of the older firefighters viewed wearing an air tank as unnecessary and even un-manly. Going inside a smoke-filled burning building without an air tank on was like a badge of courage.

They were called "smoke eaters" and rightly so. They had to crawl as low to the ground as possible to stay underneath the smoke and get to the fire. Many of the old-timers would wrap towels around their necks and use them as make-shift respirators. Still, it is virtually impossible to avoid breathing in some smoke, as well as heated air and toxic gasses. This is not only very dangerous in the moment, but also extremely hazardous to your long-term health. Many of these men developed lung cancer and heart disease. I respect the hell out of them for their courage and bravery. I really don't know if I would have been able to do the job during those times.

During the 1800s, fire engines were powered by men pumping levers on a rotating basis in order to provide an adequate, consistent supply of water through leather hoses. This was physically exhausting and required the involvement of the entire platoon of firefighters. These engines were eventually replaced by more efficient horse-drawn, steam fire engines, which were called Steamers. Most firefighters then were volunteers and, in the event of a fire, they would have to bridle the horses, then go to the fire station and hook them up to the Steamer. As they departed the firehouse, the whistle sounded and the men would run in between the horses to the fire scene, holding onto the reins and stutter stepping all the way. There were usually a couple of Dalmatian dogs; it was said that the dogs had a calming effect on the horses.

Those firefighters who did not get to the station in time had two other options for getting to the fire scene: bicycle or "shanks mare," also known as the "heel and toe express" – or, in plain English, they walked. Because of these delays, one can only imagine what kind of headway fires gained in those days.

Today's firefighters are much safer due to the improved standard operating procedures and regulations that are in place. I will always have the utmost respect for the old-school firefighters who came before us and paved the way. Because of their dedication and sacrifice, we are safer, healthier, and more knowledgeable. It is our duty to keep the good traditions in place and continue to improve our profession for the firefighters of today and generations to come.

The traditions of the department and the pride each generation has for the job is willingly passed on to all new firefighters who are respectful and eager to learn the job. East Cleveland Firefighters have always taken pride in themselves, and the traditions that were passed on through the years certainly had a lot to do with sustaining that pride.

Dispatcher: "9-1-1 What's your emergency?"

9-1-1 Caller: "I need to go to the doctor cause my food fell out and my ankle hurts."

CHAPTER 3

The Brotherhood

When you are hired as a firefighter, you also enter into a brotherhood. It is not something that happens the first day, first week, or even the first month. But after the first year, a firefighter gets a good feel for the brotherhood. By this time, he has had his first fire, his first vehicle accident, his first shooting or stabbing, and numerous other EMS and fire-related emergencies. He is under the microscope at these emergencies as well as in the engine house and is constantly being monitored and evaluated by other firefighters and officers.

New firefighters will have numerous occasions to have second thoughts about taking the job. At least that was the case in East Cleveland. They can't understand why they are sometimes treated like second-class citizens for a good portion of the first year by other firefighters, especially the senior men. Some will second-guess themselves when they go into their first fire, because nothing can fully prepare you for the feeling of entering an extremely hot, smoke-filled, unfamiliar, dangerous environment, unable to see the gloved hand in front of your face. They will also wonder if they will always have to do all of the shit details, or will always be called "boot."

The first year is critical. It's an attitude check, a time when others find out if you are a team player or not. It is your probationary period, the one year in your career when you can lose your job without much recourse due to an unfavorable evaluation by your officers. You have to prove to the other firefighters and officers that you will fit in and do this job. You are expected to talk less, listen more, and be respectful, to the officers, the other firefighters and the traditions. No one is "one of the guys" after only a short time on the job.

When you have proven yourself to the men on your shift, especially through your actions at the emergency scene, you will be accepted and gradually welcomed into the brotherhood. You will not be fully accepted by everyone at the same time. There will be some firefighters, usually the more senior veterans, who will not accept you in until they are completely confident that you are serious about the job and willing to do what it takes to uphold the traditions of the department.

A good example of this process was the interaction between East Cleveland senior firefighter Jeff Polson and new recruit Bobby Glorioso. Jeff was a big country boy, a hard-charging firefighter who was a bit rough around the edges but who respected the values and traditions of the fire service. Bob was a new man, but intelligent, physically fit, eager, respectful, basically an ideal recruit.

After about 3 months on the job, Bob excitedly informed me that Jeff had finally spoken to him for the first time. I asked him what Jeff said to him and I'll never forget his answer. Bob said that Jeff leaned over in his recliner to his left and looked him dead in the eyes and said in his raspy voice, "So are you a homo or what?" That was it… after 3 months! I had a good laugh when he told me this story but, believe it or not, those two guys became good friends. Jeff was a member of Bob's wedding party years later.

Jeff was a big, strong, country boy and 100% old school. When I was a rookie he treated me like shit, just like he did with all rookies. I honestly thought that there was a good chance that I would have to fight Jeff but eventually learned that his treatment of rookies was Jeff's way of indoctrinating new firefighters. It was most likely good for me that we didn't fight because he probably would have kicked my ass. I also became very close to Jeff and respected his love for the job and traditions of the fire service. It was a bit of "tough love" and an attitude check more than anything.

Unlike most fire departments, in East Cleveland the ratio of black and white firefighters is around fifty-fifty. The brotherhood between black and white firefighters has always been, for the most part, very strong. There were some, but not many, instances of racism. The bond is tight, more so than in most other racially mixed fire departments, particularly the Cleveland Fire Department, according to many common friends. Also, as a small department, the firefighters in East Cleveland were always working closely together and not exclusively with members of their own race. Because of this racial makeup firefighters learned about each other's cultures whether they wanted to or not. In East Cleveland, most firefighters really embraced this unique opportunity, and it evolved into a tight bond that reached well beyond the walls of the engine house. Firefighters spend 24 hours together in the firehouse every third day. The brotherhood within the department is crucial to, not only the working environment inside the engine house, but also to the performance of the crews working together at the emergency scene.

Dispatcher: "9-1-1, what's your emergency??"

9-1-1 Caller: "I've been infected with mites for over 20 years!"

CHAPTER 4

So, You Want to Be a Firefighter

In September 1988, I had nearly given up hope of working for the East Cleveland Fire Department. I'd taken the written exam and physical agility test almost two years previously, and had been waiting for a call ever since. I was 31 years old and had accepted the fact that I would have to work a 9-to-5 schedule doing a job I didn't like the rest of my life. Then they finally called!

My older brother Tim thought I was insane. He couldn't understand how anyone in his right mind, especially someone without a college degree, like me, would leave an excellent office job, as a manager, and take a $10,000 pay cut. But I was elated.

Firefighting had not been a childhood dream of mine. I'd never considered it until my mid-to late-twenties. I remembered seeing firefighters sitting outside the engine houses on sunny days, watching people go by. They always looked happy and relaxed. And getting paid to sleep between calls sounded pretty good to me! Sure, they had to put out fires, but that had to beat the hell out of wearing a tie and carrying a briefcase into an office every day. That tie was choking the life out of me.

The polygraph test was my biggest concern. I was no street thug, but I wasn't a choir boy either. My cousin was already working for the East Cleveland Fire Department and he briefed me on what to expect. He was also the union president and was privy to the list of questions that I would be asked in the interview session. To this day, I do not feel guilty about this competitive edge during the interview process. I wanted to do everything possible to get this job and retire forever from the 9-to-5 business world that I was a part of.

The day for the polygraph came and I drove to the East Cleveland Police Department. I sat down in the test chair and waited for the detective to come in and hook me up. As I sat down, my mind raced. My cousin had informed me that the goal of the tester was to determine through the examination whether a candidate was honest. Equally as important, they wanted to determine if a candidate was a thief, a drug abuser, or a sexual deviant. Almost everyone in my high school class, including me, had at least tried marijuana. That was over ten years prior, but I hoped that the question wouldn't come up.

The detective entered the room with a clipboard and sat in a chair in front of me. He seemed like a real hard-ass. I was nervous. He proceeded to ask me a long list of questions, many of which pertained to those three things that will get you eliminated. Some of the questions were repeated, possibly in an attempt to look for consistency. In my earlier years, I had stolen a few things but nothing big, and nothing in my adult years. I wasn't too concerned about being classified as a thief. The same was true for the sexual deviant thing. Getting falsely labeled as a "drug abuser" seemed like the one thing that could possibly prevent me from my getting this job.

After the questions, the detective hooked the electrical leads onto me and began the polygraph test. As the test began I remembered seeing a movie where a guy beat the polygraph by putting a rock in his shoe. When he answered each question he pressed on the rock with his foot, and supposedly the sharp pain would take his mind off the question and confuse the examiner. I didn't know if this really worked but I made a weak effort to duplicate the action, without the rock, on the first couple of questions. I knew that this was stupid and I quickly abandoned this technique. I nervously finished answering the questions. Surprisingly, this part of the test took only about ten minutes, and then it was over.

As it turned out, my worries were for nothing. The examiner jokingly told me that he'd seen much worse than me. It was as if a huge weight had been lifted off my shoulders. I knew now that I was going to start my new career. At 31 years of age, I had previously worked in over ten different jobs. This would be the last, and I couldn't wait to get started.

Dispatcher: "9-1-1, what's your emergency??"

9-1-1 caller: "I need an ambulance, a Black & Mild, and a cold pop. No, make that a cigarette and a cold pop."

(Actual 9-1-1 call)

CHAPTER 5

First Day in the Hood

John D. Rockefeller once had a home in East Cleveland, a small city – less than three square miles – just outside Cleveland, Ohio. Through the mid-20th century, it was affluent and mostly white. But as black residents moved in, whites departed for more distant suburbs; the term "white flight" could have been coined there.

By 1988, the population of 27,000 was mostly poor, and the city was riddled with crime and blight. Steel burglar bars on exterior windows were commonplace. Bulletproof glass in convenience stores, gas stations, and carryout restaurants was the norm, not the exception. Gangs ruled the streets, selling crack cocaine on street corners, and the city became one of the most violent in Ohio. The understaffed police department was faced with a tremendous workload. East Cleveland police officer John Bechtel, who was also the union president, was quoted in the newspaper as saying, "It will be safer in Iraq than it will be in East Cleveland if more police officers are not hired." But 1988 was also the year the city was declared a fiscal disaster and taken over by the state, after many years of inept, and corrupt local government.

There were a couple of run-down, cheap hotels infested with prostitutes, drug abusers, and long-term residents. The hotel managers in East Cleveland operated like slumlords. They collected rent but when it came to providing maintenance and comfortable living spaces, they did the bare minimum, sometimes less. Some were prosecuted for housing violations, and more should have been. They didn't keep the buildings up to code and they were often hard to contact, or altogether unavailable.

Most of the homes in East Cleveland are large, older, and solidly built, reminders of the city's past. They are the kind of homes that we don't see much now, with beautiful wood trim throughout. But the years had taken their toll, and those owned by landlords and rented to poor tenants were often neglected. As a result, they became fire hazards.

The rate of structure fires in East Cleveland was significantly higher than in the neighboring suburban cities, and on par with the worst neighborhoods in Cleveland, a city of nearly 400,000 residents. The arson rate was also high and when the houses burned, they burned well, due to the balloon frame type construction, with no fire stops built into the structure. As a new firefighter, I was informed that there would be a lot of fires. Being young and eager, this excited me. I couldn't wait to get started.

Our work schedule was one day (24 hours) on, two days (48 hours) off. And every third week we got five consecutive days off. I couldn't believe this schedule. I was as happy as a pig in slop and I had to pinch myself to remind me that this was, indeed, a reality.

I found out that I would only have one duty day on shift before I went to the fire cadet academy. It was not unusual for a new man in East Cleveland to work months on shift before going to cadet school. It just so happened to work out this way for me. In a way, I was actually glad because I didn't know anything about firefighting or the fire service. I didn't even know the difference between a fire engine and a ladder truck. I needed to get to the academy so I wouldn't look so stupid to my co-workers when I returned. I just needed to get this one day out of the way.

I started my first drive to work from my home in Akron to Interstate 77 North, through the Cleveland inner belt, around "Dead Man's Curve," along the east shore way of Lake Erie on I-90 East. I exited onto Eddy Road and turned right, making my way through East Cleveland. I remember seeing a vacant house that had been stripped of half the aluminum siding. I'd never seen this before, but would learn later that this was a common occurrence. Same with the theft of copper pipe. I continued on Eddy Road, passing overgrown vacant lots filled with trash and old tires, abandoned buildings scarred with graffiti, and a sign that announced, "Welcome to East Cleveland, a city on the rise."

I reached Euclid Avenue and turned left. A minute later I turned right onto Beersford Avenue then turned left into the city parking lot that the police and fire department shared with the other city employees. I found a spot then walked through the doors to the fire station for the first time, in October of 1988.

I found out very quickly that a new man didn't even have a name at first. I was referred to as "boot" and the veteran firefighters didn't talk to boots very often unless it was job-related. I initially hated being called boot but did not let anyone know this. I knew that there would be a one-year probationary period, so I just kept my mouth shut and did what was expected without complaint.

Boots were watched to see what kind of attitude they had, and how eager they were to learn the job and do the lousy details without complaining. They were watched to see if they had a problem taking direction or being a team player. Boots were supposed to do a lot of listening and not much talking. Boots were treated in this manner until they proved themselves in the engine house and, more important, at the ultimate proving ground, the fire scene. I didn't mind paying my dues, even though I came in ten years older than most boots when they start their careers. Hell, I had so many bad jobs in the past that these boot rules weren't going to bother me. I killed chickens in a slaughterhouse when I was younger and it doesn't get much worse than that. At the end of each day I was covered in chicken shit and blood and I smelled like a rotten feedbag.

The bigger challenge for me was to learn this job and become confident in my abilities. I wanted to get through this first day without any fires and get on to fire cadet school to learn the basics. Well, it didn't quite work out that way.

Shortly after lunch we received a call reporting a house fire with visible flames coming from the first floor. Like it or not, I was going to get my rookie baptism my first day on the job. When the alarm bells sounded my heart was racing. I was extremely nervous because I didn't have a clue as to what I was supposed to do. Earlier that morning a couple of the newer recruit firefighters had given me a short training class on how to put on the turnout gear and breathing apparatus. My biggest concern was being able to put on the air mask correctly, but I didn't really think that they would expect me to go inside the structure.

I got dressed as fast as I could because I had been told to never make the crew wait. I was made aware that the East Cleveland Fire Department took great pride in response time and aggressive interior firefighting. They told me to never forget those two things if I expected to become a good firefighter. I jumped on the back of Truck 121 and five seconds later we were rolling, lights on, sirens and air horns blasting. My adrenaline was pumping like crazy and the feeling was exhilarating. We were going through red lights and everybody was getting out of our way. The feeling was amazing!

I looked over at veteran firefighter Rich Kaleal and he looked as cool as a cucumber. His confidence was reassuring. I did my best to calm down, but I was still pretty jacked up.

We pulled up to the scene and I saw smoke and flames coming from a first-floor window. I was still fumbling with my breathing apparatus, making adjustments to the straps, oblivious to the fact that the attack of this fire was already in progress. Through radio communication, all three crews were coordinating the water supply, hose line placement, ventilation, and search & rescue operations that were necessary for this fire attack. Suddenly I heard the officer in charge say, "Take the new guy inside." I thought to myself, "Oh shit, here we go!"

Kaleal approached me and said "Mask up kid, we're going to the second floor to check for fire extension." I put my air mask on, opened the valve to the air bottle, and tightened the straps, reasonably sure that I had properly masked up. I followed Kaleal through the back door, with firefighter Mick Gunn close behind me. I was amazed that I couldn't even see my gloved hand in front of my face because of the thick smoke. I had no idea how Kaleal was going to proceed. They didn't need to remind me to stay close because I wasn't going to let him get away from me. I would have been lost if we were separated.

We proceeded up the second-floor stairway. I felt the heat, but it didn't seem very intense. Later I learned that the fire had been contained to the kitchen area only; the veterans dismissed it as a "training burn." But for me it was an excellent way to start my career. I had passed my first test. I didn't freak out in the smoke-filled environment. I loved the adrenaline rush and was very anxious to experience it again. The transition from office manager to firefighter had started out on a great note.

Paramedic: "Why do you have Vaseline all over your body?"

Patient: "I was going over to my girlfriend's house, ya know what I'm saying, so I needed to be slippery. I got to get my nuts out the sandbox!"

(Actual EMS run)

CHAPTER 6

Fire School

The time needed to complete Cadet Fire Academy varies from department to department. In East Cleveland, school was six weeks of learning the basics in almost every aspect of firefighting. I didn't agree with the premise then and, after more than 20 years, I'm even more convinced now that they don't teach new recruits properly at fire school.

Instead of teaching new recruits a little bit of everything, they should concentrate on teaching them how to fight fires. Many things, such as fire investigation, fire behavior, fire safety inspections, fire apparatus operation (hydraulics), and various other subjects, really don't need to be taught to new recruits. Recruits need to learn how to become proficient in firefighting before branching out into other areas.

The new men in most departments, especially busy departments, will spend their first few years almost exclusively on the backs of engines or ladder trucks. They will be doing the grunt work on the attack hose lines. They will be inside the burning structures pulling ceilings down, opening up walls, and chasing fire. They'll be doing search and rescue, ventilation, and water supply operations. Those are the things new recruits need to learn, through classroom and practical drills. Sometimes the powers that be over-analyze and make things more complex than they need to be. Because decisions have to be made quickly on the fire ground, it is best to keep things clear and simple, rather than throwing out fancy jargon that is not familiar to everyone. Keep it simple: Teach new recruits how to fight fires.

Although I needed training desperately, I couldn't wait to finish fire school. As a matter of fact, I hated it. It was a little like being back in high school. The nine-hour day seemed to drag on. I didn't really care for most of the instructors and some of my classmates were real ass-kissers.

Before I had started fire school, one of the veteran firefighters in East Cleveland said, "Hey Mike, you have one fire under your belt and that's more than most of the instructors who teach at fire school." East Cleveland Deputy Chief Jerry Kirchner, a Navy man affectionately referred to as the "Sea Hag," told me to "just get through fire school then come back and learn how to fight fires the East Cleveland way." These comments really meant something to me. I understood that when I got back to East Cleveland I would be learning from experienced, well-respected firefighters who knew what they were doing. This made me feel good about joining one of the busiest, yet lowest paid, fire departments in Ohio.

The instructors were from suburban departments, and as I'd been told, had limited firefighting experience. The one instructor who stood out to me was a Captain from a suburban department who thought that he was a bad-ass. Let's just call him Captain X.

On our first day of class, Captain X walked in fifteen minutes late, unshaven, his hair was a mess, wearing an untucked flannel shirt and blue jeans. His first words were, "You ladies will be all right if you're not a bunch of fuck heads!" I immediately lost all respect for this guy. He talked like he had fought countless fires and was a hard-charging interior firefighter. I found out later that despite 25 years of experience, he'd actually fought very few fires. I also learned that true bad-asses didn't brag about it, and they carried themselves much differently.

At the end of my first week, Captain X called off sick and went duck hunting. He was the only instructor out of ten or so who gave me low grades. I think it was personal. He even questioned, on paper, my desire to become a firefighter, and that really bothered me. It might have had something to do with the fact that I wasn't kissing his ass like a few others in my class were. I wasn't disruptive or disrespectful, but I surely was not going to be a suck up to this guy.

When our Fire Chief asked me about the low marks that Captain X gave me, I could only answer honestly: "Chief, the guy's just an asshole, plain and simple." He must have known about the guy because he just kind of smirked and let it go at that. If I saw Captain X today, I wouldn't hold a grudge. I had no hard feelings. He probably made me work even harder by doubting my resolve and my love for this job.

The only other thing that stood out in fire school was the major fire in Cleveland Heights, which borders East Cleveland. We were on break from the classroom and I overheard instructors talking about what they were hearing on a portable radio. There was a large fire on Coventry Road in Cleveland Heights, and the city was calling for aid from other nearby fire departments. I'll never forget what I heard next. An instructor said, "They just called for an engine from East Cleveland. Those guys are fucking animals. When they come in they just take over the fire scene."

I didn't say anything but, deep inside, I was proud. I was going to a city where firefighters had a great reputation. I was going to East Cleveland and I couldn't wait to get there!

Paramedic to prison inmate: "We have a rule that if your vital signs are ok we don't have to take you to the hospital. Sign here!"

CHAPTER 7

In House

A firefighter will usually spend more than 80 percent of each 24-hour duty day inside the engine house. The engine house is our residence, our safe-haven, our "home away from home." It is the place we spend almost one-fourth of our lives. Yes, we can relax and even sleep at the engine house when on duty, but it's not the same as at home. In the back of our minds, we know the alarm bells can sound at any time.

In East Cleveland we start the day at 8:30 A.M. Prior to that time, all platoon members are expected to sign the journal, place their turnout gear next to their assigned apparatus, and test their SCBA device to ensure that it's working properly and that the air tank is full. This is arguably the most important daily equipment check that a firefighter performs, but there are many firefighters who don't check it until after the morning meeting (me, a few times), and some who don't check it at all. The SCBA is your lifeline when inside a toxic environment. It's really foolish for a firefighter to disregard this simple equipment check.

Showing up late, even one minute, for the 8:30 A.M. meeting is not tolerated unless you called and asked for another firefighter to hold over for you until you arrive. If not, you are considered AWOL and will most likely be written up and disciplined. I always thought that the lateness rules were a bit severe. There was one instance when Lieutenant Bobby Jenkins was AWOL for the first time in about twenty years. Believe it or not, he was written up and forced to forfeit a vacation day. I thought that was ridiculous, especially since the rule was not consistently enforced.

I always believed that writing someone up should be the last resort. As a matter of fact, I would do my best to cover for guys who were late, as long as it wasn't a common occurrence. Most guys agreed with that line of thinking and would cover for each other. But there were always a few officers who couldn't wait for a guy to come in late so they could write him up. There always seemed to be a couple of guys who couldn't be trusted.

At the morning meeting, the lieutenant reads the run schedule so that all personnel know their assignments for that shift. In a small department, your riding assignment can change each duty day. You might be riding on the ambulance one day, driving the ladder truck the next, then assigned on the back of the pumper the day after that. In many of the large fire departments, like Cleveland or Akron, assignments can last a year, sometimes longer. In East Cleveland, we do not have the luxury of surplus manpower, so we cannot specialize. Our firefighters need to be well versed in all aspects of firefighting – apparatus driver/engineer, fire attack, ventilation/search & rescue, and EMS. For this reason, I would put an East Cleveland firefighter up against any in the country to compare raw ability and skill level. I may be biased, but I know that some firefighters from other nearby departments, who know our reputation, would agree. Our guys are extremely skilled, confident, and aggressive.

After reading the riding assignments, the lieutenant will review the schedule for the day. This could be training, inspections, details, or my personal favorite, holiday routine (all details suspended because it is a Holiday). The details are normally assigned to the recruit firefighters who get most of the shit details.

After the schedule is read, night watches are assigned to four firefighters, according to seniority. We did not have the luxury of full-time dispatchers so we had to handle this task with on duty firefighters. If we all went on a call, we were able to switch the phones over to the police dispatcher. The nighttime dispatching slots, from 10 P.M. until 8:30 A.M. the next day, had to be covered. The senior men usually take the first and last slots. New guys get stuck with the 1:00 A.M. to 3:15 A.M. and the 3:15 A.M. to 5:30 A.M. shifts, which really mess up your sleep habits.

I was a bit lucky, however, to have a guy named Gary Warren on my shift when I was new. Gary would take the first shift but, almost like clockwork, an hour or so in, he would start nodding off. I would wait until he banged the back of his head on the wall, then walk over and ask if he would like to trade watches. He always agreed and sometimes even thanked me. I was a night owl, so it worked great for me. It was one of the few times that I got the best of a senior man, no disrespect intended!

The night watches have always been a handicap for us, but we've never been able to negotiate them over to the police department dispatchers on a permanent basis. It was always about money, or specifically, the lack of it. It's not what's best for us or our citizens, but compromises keep the city afloat.

Morning meetings used to include run reviews. That policy, unfortunately, has fallen by the wayside. In run reviews, we would discuss all of the calls from the previous day, even false alarms. Much of it was repetitive, but that's how things become cemented in our memories. Like the old Shaolin monk saying, "When the fist strikes 1,000 times, it becomes natural."

Run reviews were dropped from the morning routine when the department transitioned from typing "run cards" on a typewriter to entering the information into a computer. The Fire Chief at that time was a good example of the Peter Principle, someone getting promoted beyond his level of competence. He also had a huge ego, and would not listen to veteran firefighters who wanted to keep this valuable training tool. Now the only time that we review runs is when the previous shift had an unusual fire or EMS call, a rescue or a shooting.

The morning meeting is conducted in a very laid back, low-key environment. Most guys ease into the meeting by grabbing a cup of coffee and reading the sports page from the Cleveland Plain Dealer just prior to the meeting. The officers and senior firefighters are seated comfortably in the padded recliners and the new recruits are seated in the "boot pound." The name was coined by then Firefighter Rick Wilcox, after the "dog pound," the section in the Cleveland Browns' stadium for the craziest, most die-hard fans. The boot pound is a row of four or five old, beat-up, uncomfortable chairs that face toward the recliners and away from the big screen T.V. It's another test, and the worst thing that a recruit could do would be to show that he was upset about being forced to sit in the boot pound. That would be like exposing a wound and asking to have salt thrown into it.

There is no set time when the morning meeting is over, and after that, things are pretty loose. A 10 A.M. training might start closer to 10:30. I'm not sure how other departments operate, but aside from morning meeting and responding to calls, punctuality is not a priority in East Cleveland. This may seem unprofessional, but it's a welcome break from the speed required for emergencies. When the business of the day is finished, we will usually grab a second cup of coffee and talk sports, or what we're eating for lunch or dinner, or what we did on our off-duty days, or any topic under the sun. It's a nice way to ease into the work day.

After the morning meeting, the apparatus and equipment are checked and the vehicles are cleaned. For many years, the trucks were sponged off with water every day, even when they were clean. Thankfully, this tradition has died off and the apparatus are now cleaned only when needed. Although there are probably many old-school firefighters who don't agree, it seems to make a whole lot more sense to me.

Next is housework. The junior men will do most of the housework, including all of the least desirable jobs like cleaning the toilets.

We usually take a morning break around 10 A.M. On rare occasions, on weekends or holidays when there is nothing on the schedule and we don't get any calls, those breaks can last until 8:30 A.M. the next day. What a job! You gotta love it!

People have asked me what else a firefighter does to pass the time during a long 24-hour shift. We can work out in the weight room. Most departments, including ours in East Cleveland, have just about everything needed for physical fitness in cardio and weight machines, as well as free weights. Most firefighters bring their laptop computers and spend a lot of time watching TV and on the Internet. Others kill time by reading, playing cards, board games or video games. In my early years, I sometimes felt like we were getting paid to goof off – and I loved it!

Firefighters definitely sleep on the job and are encouraged to do so, especially the guys assigned to the ambulances. Many shifts they run calls all night and don't sleep a wink after midnight. I always encourage them to sleep whenever possible.

One night I didn't get to sleep until 11:30 P.M. after a fairly busy day flowing fire hydrants and doing other details in the hot summer sun. Just as I got to sleep, we received a call for a house fire. We worked that house fire from midnight until 2:30 A.M. Just as we were finishing up we received another call for an apartment fire, and worked that fire from 2:30 A.M. until 5. We were all mentally and physically exhausted but still could not sleep until all of the air bottles were filled, equipment was checked, and reports were generated. At this point your body is beat up and you are running on fumes and eagerly awaiting the shift change. After a night like that it takes almost two days for your body to fully recover.

Because of this, I am a huge proponent of the "power nap." I have even ordered firefighters to take a mandatory two-hour power nap or get written up. You just never know what might happen, so you need to rest whenever possible. We are paid to respond to emergencies and we need to be as fit as possible in order to do the best for our citizens. Most firefighters wouldn't mind fighting fires and answering EMS calls during regular business hours. Unfortunately, it doesn't work that way, and never will.

Dispatcher to 9-1-1 caller: "You said she's worried about the unborn baby's health, but she's been smoking crack for the last four days.... Oh, she also had a beer this morning too?"

(Actual 9-1-1 call)

CHAPTER 8

War Stories – Introducing Charlie Catania

Firefighters' war stories run the entire gamut of emotions. Some are tragic. Some are funny. Some are heartwarming. War stories are what firefighters talk about at golf outings, cookouts, parties, retirement dinners, or when they belly up to a bar over a couple of cold beers.

Some guys willingly share their experiences. As a matter of fact, it's hard to get some guys to stop talking. Like Captain Charlie Catania. Charlie was a great guy. He spent his entire career in East Cleveland, then unexpectedly passed away in 2010, only a few years into his retirement.

I dreaded the funeral services but understood that the family needed to heal. At his wake I read a two-page letter describing my respect for this great man. I'd rather run into a burning building than speak in front of people, but I had to pay tribute to my friend.

Charlie was well-liked and respected by both the black and white firefighters, which wasn't always the case, especially for officers. He taught me a lot and he was an excellent fire boss. But the thing I liked best about Charlie was that he was such a funny son of a bitch. When he was on duty the mood was upbeat. He loved to bust balls and tell jokes and would talk to anyone who would listen. For hours. We joked about trying not to make eye contact with him, because once you did, you were trapped in his spider web of monologue.

His stories were not dull but sometimes repetitive, and always very long. Some of the veteran firefighters, who had worked with Charlie for years, would get up in the middle of one of his stories, not caring about being rude, and walk away without saying a word. Charlie would carry on with whoever was still there. Or he would get up and follow the guy, to the bathroom or wherever, talking the entire time. Sometimes we wished for an emergency or a phone call in order to escape. But the bottom line was that he kept things upbeat and made people laugh. Charlie was a hell of a man, a hell of a firefighter, and a hell of an officer!

Whenever the veteran firefighters or retirees started telling war stories, the rookies listened. War stories are not only entertaining, but they are also a tremendous learning tool. Their lessons will not be found in text books. War stories are one of the great things we take with us when we retire. They are unique events that can never be duplicated or taken away.

Paramedic: "Are you allergic to anything?"

Patient: "Yeah, blond-haired, blue-eyed honkies!"

(Actual EMS run)

CHAPTER 9

War Story 2: Lakefront Fire

The call came in at 2:30 A.M. It was a hot Summer night in August, 1991. I remember this clearly because I was on dispatch duty at station one. The frantic female caller screamed, "My damn house is on fire! Hurry up, you gotta hurry, please!" I could hear the panic and distress in her voice. She gave me the address but hung up before I could tell her to get everyone out of the house.

My heart was pounding as I pressed the hot line button to alert the four firefighters who made up the crew of Engine 112, at station two. I then turned on the house lights, automatically opened the trap doors that covered the access hole to the poles, then activated the station house alarm bells to wake up the remaining seven firefighters and officers.

As the Deputy Chief came down the stairs and into the apparatus room, I informed him that we had a report of a working house fire on Lakefront Street. The phones were ringing off the hook as we dressed, another indication that this was not a false alarm. In less than one minute we were all on board the trucks with "wheels rolling."

At this time, we were responding with twelve men, manning two engines and a ladder truck. The Deputy Chief was the officer in charge, and he responded with Ladder Truck 121 and took command of the fire scene upon the trucks' arrival. Our other pumper was Engine 114. I was assigned to ride on the back of Engine 114 and on this day, we would be the first arriving apparatus on scene.

We made the right turn from Euclid Avenue onto Lakefront and could see heavy smoke hovering in the street, making visibility difficult for the driver. The smoke was so thick that we couldn't initially tell which house was on fire. Smoke at street level is usually an indicator that there is fire in the basement or on the first floor. We reached the address of the caller who reported the fire and, sure enough, heavy flames were blowing out a rear window on the first floor. Thick, dark brown smoke was pouring out of the second and third floor windows and roof eaves, indicating that the fire had, most likely, extended upward to the second floor and possibly the third-floor attic.

The officer in charge radioed all personnel to inform them that there was a citizen report that all residents of the house had made it outside. This was a relief; we could concentrate on attacking the fire, as opposed to search and rescue operations. But rescue still needed to be our first priority, just in case we were given bad information.

Engine 114 Captain Charlie Catania called for a pre-connected one-and-three-quarter-inch hose line to attack the fire on the first floor. Truck 121 crew initiated exterior ventilation, knocking out the upper-floor windows by dropping a ground ladder into them. This technique can take out a lot of windows quickly. Engine 112 crew took a second pre-connected one-and-three-quarter-inch hose line to the second floor where the fire had already extended. After ventilating the exterior windows, Truck 121 crew masked up and checked for fire extension into the attic.

In East Cleveland we rarely cut ventilation holes in roofs. Vertical ventilation holes are very effective, but when you respond with only twelve firefighters, you look at strategy differently. Having the luxury of manpower enables fire crews to perform operations that they otherwise would be unable to. We normally ventilated horizontally through windows and doors. The City of Cleveland Fire Department, for example, almost always cuts holes in roofs, but they may have twenty to thirty firefighters respond on an initial alarm, if needed.

This house was very large and, from front to back, unusually deep. Our three-man crew from Engine 114 took the hose line in through the front door and headed toward the rear. The plan was to push the fire out the back windows. Attacking it from the rear of the house would have spread it around inside.

Visibility was zero. We could feel the heat but couldn't see the glow of the fire yet. We had to first crawl through the living room and dining room. The difference in the temperature when crawling, as opposed to standing, is hundreds of degrees. We inched our way toward the kitchen, dodging furniture along the way. We eventually saw the orange glow and heard the crackling of the flames. That moment is always a relief. You can finally start throwing water and darkening down the flames, which alleviates some of the intense heat.

We knocked down the fire in the kitchen, only to discover that it had extended upward via a rear staircase. We could hear flames popping and the ceiling falling as a solid wall of fire rolled upward toward the second floor. We knocked down the fire in the lower section of the stairway but had to stop when our air bottles went into alarm, indicating that it was time to get out and get fresh ones. The fire was not extinguished, but we knew that another crew was already in place on the second floor.

The Engine 112 crew were able to extinguish the flames at the top of the staircase before they needed additional air bottles. But fire still raged in a second-floor bedroom and threatened to find its way into the attic.

When my crew and I had changed our air bottles, we returned to the first floor to overhaul the kitchen and staircase. There was still a lot of heat there, but we were now able to stand and open up the walls and ceiling to find hidden flames. When all the hot spots were under control, we then proceeded outside for a third air bottle. At this point we were completely exhausted and hoped that we didn't have to go back inside immediately. All of my undergarments were drenched in sweat.

Truck 121 crew reported that the fire had extended to the attic, and deployed a third hose line there. They knocked down the fire in the attic without much trouble then, to increase visibility, began ventilating the smoke by pointing the hose line out toward the top of a window and using a wide pattern fog stream of water to pull the smoke through the window and to the outside air.

Engine 112 crew attempted to return to the second-floor rear bedroom, but flames had kicked up again in the second-floor kitchen. They opened up the walls and ceiling in the kitchen and extinguished the flames for good this time. By the time they could advance their hose line to the rear bedroom, it was almost fully involved with flame. Engine 112 crew knocked down the majority of the flames but then had to retreat for more air bottles. They radioed to Deputy Chief Jerry Kirchner, a.k.a. "Sea Hag," that a crew was needed to finish knocking the fire in the second-floor rear bedroom.

The Sea Hag told Captain Catania to take a couple guys up there and knock that fire. Catania told me and Firefighter Curtis Jackson to go with him. We masked up and made our way up a front staircase to the second floor. Visibility was still almost zero. We followed the hose line that had been deployed by Engine 112 crew and crawled to the rear bedroom. The door to the bedroom was closed, and the nozzle was lying in front of it.

Captain Catania radioed to the Sea Hag to have someone bring up a pike pole, a tool used for opening up ceilings. We then opened the door. We felt heat but quickly determined that most of the fire was in the walls and ceiling. Jackson had the nozzle and I started to open up the walls with my axe. My strength was pretty much gone, so my efforts were slow. But we saw that most of the fire was in the ceiling anyway, so we backed out, closed the door and waited for the pike pole.

Jackson opened up the hose line nozzle on the ceiling above in an attempt to cool us off as we waited. But the heat was too great and the water provided very little cooling.

A firefighter brought us the pike pole, and we opened the door and started pulling the ceiling down. My low-air alarm began to vibrate. This meant I had approximately five more minutes before my air tank was empty. Foolishly, I worked for another a minute or so before informing my crew that I had to leave. I dropped down to crawl, using the hose line to guide me out. I was completely spent, physically and mentally.

Even on the floor, visibility was still so low that I never saw the other firefighter crawling toward me until we bumped into each other. Navigating around each other wasted more time and air. Once clear, I knew that I just had to make it to the top of the stairs, then I was home free.

Or so I thought. What happened next gave me that feeling of "impending doom" that I had heard about at the fire training academy.

The hose line that I was following went off to the left — not the way I thought it should be going. We were taught that if you follow the female couplings on the hose line it will eventually lead you outside, but I also had seen hose lines piled up like spaghetti inside of buildings. And to make matters worse, the hose that was going to the attic was going up the same staircase that ours was. It would be so easy to get confused, especially when you can't see and know that you are running out of air.

My mind started racing and I was getting close to freaking out. I thought of the stories that I'd heard of firefighters getting disoriented and never making it outside. Then I remembered my training and tried to relax and compose myself. I recalled someone saying that "cooler heads will prevail." This helped, but it didn't give me a solution. The anxiety quickly returned and I knew that I had to choose right or left immediately before I ran out of air.

Like a gift from God, I suddenly saw the smoky image of a firefighter walking past me in the direction to the right, where I had initially intended to go. It was Captain Catania and I immediately followed him. Sure enough, the top of the stairs was only ten feet away from where I had been kneeling. By this time, I was so exhausted that I felt like falling down the stairs because I wasn't sure if I had the strength to walk down. When I got outside I collapsed on the lawn and just laid there for about ten minutes, not speaking a word. I thought about how that could have ended very differently. Apparently, it just wasn't my time.

After that fire on Lakefront, my perspective changed drastically. No longer did I feel like I got paid to "do nothing." No longer did I feel the least bit guilty about taking my paycheck. No longer did I buy into the perception that firemen mostly just sit in chairs outside the engine house and watch the people go by. I realized then and there that firemen are not paid to do busy work as part of their daily work routine. They respond to emergencies from which they might not return.

I also grew quite a bit as a firefighter that day. I learned to pay greater attention to potential hazards and escape routes on the fire scene. I took a more analytical and less reckless approach to the scene. I realized that keeping myself and my fellow firefighters safe was the top priority, although it isn't always portrayed in that manner. The standard line that is depicted in most firefighting textbooks is that the number one goal of firefighters is to protect citizen lives and property. After this fire, I knew that the number one, unwritten goal, is to protect the lives of firefighters first, then citizen lives, then property, in that order. If a firefighter tells you any different, he's lying.

I appreciated being alive more that day than I ever had before in my 34 years on this Earth. It was a powerful experience, my first, but not my last, brush with death.

Intoxicated patient to firefighters: "If I wasn't 78 years old, I'd rape all three of you!"

(Actual EMS run)

CHAPTER 10

Black & White

In the 1930s and '40s, the citizen population of East Cleveland was almost all white, and so was its fire department. When I started working there in 1988, the city was almost entirely black, but the fire department employed roughly equal numbers of blacks and whites. Although the city administration never said so publicly, we sensed that they would prefer that the fire department reflect the racial makeup of the citizen population.

Early on in my career I actually heard a black officer, who was nicknamed "Hurricane Bob," verbalize this at a union meeting in 1990. Being a new man, I didn't feel comfortable speaking out in regard to his statement. His comment made me feel uneasy, as if the black guys wanted to get rid of the white guys. I soon found out that this was not the case. Most guys embraced the diversity of our department, because it was rare. There were minor race issues infrequently but, for the most part, we all got along pretty damn well.

I know for fact that some firefighters, blacks and whites, voted according to color on some union issues, such as the election of executive board members. That was disappointing. In my mind it was like the "one step forward, two steps back" in race relations. At ECFD, race was always at the forefront but never divided us. We were "brothers from other mothers."

There were a few firefighters who liked to create controversy. In 2005, a decorative patch for department-issued t-shirts became fodder for one of them. The patch bore a "spitfire" symbol of a red flame surrounded by black smoke. Somehow this was turned into a racial issue by one guy. To this day, other than the symbol being black in color, I am not sure what reason he had for thinking that this spitfire was, in any way, racially offensive. But the arguments got very heated. Amazingly, it even went as far as polling the entire department to determine how many thought the symbol was offensive. As it turned out, there were two, including the one who started the controversy. Ironically, he had once referred to the guy who supported him as "a sneeze away from being retarded" – a line that became infamous within the department.

This same black firefighter was also offended when a white firefighter referred to a watermelon as a "jungle pickle." I'd never heard this before and I thought that it was somewhat comical. If you think about it logically, everything grows big in the jungle. The guy really didn't mean anything derogatory by saying it but, again, something was made out of nothing. This one didn't get heated and actually the firefighters, both black and white, got a pretty good laugh out of it and now many of them frequently refer to watermelon as "jungle pickle."

In the fire service you can't have thin skin. And the beauty of working in a racially mixed environment like East Cleveland is that black guys and white guys can say things to each other that, to outsiders, might normally cause a fight. Then they laugh about it and go drink a beer together.

Compared to most integrated fire departments, especially Cleveland's, we worked together well.

Food is frequently a hot topic of fire department discussion. We had a black firefighter named Dave Worley ("Dee-Bo") who was a pretty good cook. One day he threw together a meal that I thought was fairly unusual. The dinner consisted of beans only. He mixed in a few different types of beans and seasonings and let the pot simmer for a couple hours. The black guys and a few of the white firefighters tore those beans up. They absolutely loved that meal. I can be a picky eater, but I have learned to expand my horizons and try different foods. I am now a proud participant in the department fish fries. I have also learned to enjoy the cornbread. I finally tried Dee-Bo's greens and liked them. But there are just some foods that I won't even try.

There is no way I will ever eat "chitlins" (short for chitterlings, which are pig intestines). I am told that they're very good if you clean them correctly. Man, you could clean those stinky things forever and I will never put one in my mouth. "Chitlins" remind me of some of the nasty stuff people eat on the TV show Fear Factor. I'm not eating pig feet, ham hocks, neck bones, chicken feet, or grits, either. Still, I was told by one of the black firefighters that I'm an "honorary brother" because I eat so much chicken. I now use hot sauce frequently on chicken, especially the wings. I also love barbequed ribs, and thanks to Firefighter Rod "Big Paw" Hairston, I learned how to cook ribs so that they're "fall off the bone" tender.

When I started in the department, I was disappointed to learn that the firefighters didn't cook and eat meals together, except on certain holidays. It was pretty much "every man for himself," fast food, or a couple guys might share a meal. Looking back, I think the main reason for the change was the integration of black firefighters into the formerly all-white department, which happened before my tenure, and the gradual addition of younger, more open-minded white firefighters too. A young white firefighter named Chad Johns took on the job of cooking each meal and making sure that we all ate together. It was one of the best things that ever happened to our department.

At the dinner table, we normally join hands while our most religious firefighter blesses the table with a quick prayer. We understood that we had men with different religious beliefs, and some who did not believe, at the table, but we respected all and prayed together.

Even though it is common for us and we probably take it for granted, eating dinner at a racially mixed table is something that most people may never experience. There are differences, but in the really important areas that make up each human being – pride, respect, integrity, love of family, loyalty, and bravery – we are very much alike.

There are certain areas where, no doubt about it, our cultures are quite different. Black firefighters always seemed to be more outspoken and louder than white firefighters. They speak openly and wear their hearts on their sleeves. They will get in your face if they think that you've challenged or ridiculed them. They also laugh out loud more than white firefighters do. I've learned not to be offended if a black guy refers to me, jokingly, as a "muthafucka." One firefighter explained, "If we don't call you muthafucka, then we don't like you." I thought that was pretty funny!

Black firefighters can get very loud, especially a group of guys sitting at a table, busting balls and telling jokes. This can be annoying to those who find solace in a quiet, peaceful atmosphere, especially when a good movie is on the television! In my younger years it bothered me somewhat, but I got accustomed to it. I realized that it's better to hear laughter than complaining, so you roll with the punches and try not to sweat the small stuff.

Even though there were many great relationships established between black and white firefighters in East Cleveland, a dividing line remains. This is most evident at off-duty social events. Throughout the years the Christmas parties in the Flats of Cleveland, the golf outings, retirement parties, and cookouts were attended mostly by the white firefighters. I don't know how many times I heard the comment "Where's all the brothers?" or "How come the brothers never come to these things?" I can't say for sure why they didn't participate, because they sure as hell were welcome, and the black guys who did show up seemed to have a great time with the rest of us. On the other side of the coin, the cabarets or parties that were hosted by the black firefighters were mostly attended by the black firefighters, and a few whites. I believe that this is about preferring to stay in our comfort zones.

The black and white firefighters did get along very well for the most part, however there were obstacles and challenges along the way that disrupted the atmosphere within the firehouse walls. The single most divisive roadblock to harmonious race relations was an organization called B-Force.

B-Force was founded by and exclusively for black firefighters. Although our rules and regulations stated that no internal clubs or organizations are permitted within the department, B-Force had been in existence for over thirty years.

In my opinion, B-Force was racist, divisive, and detrimental to the department. The fact that the city administration allowed the organization to exist was a kick in the nuts to the white firefighters. Not only did it lower the morale of the white firefighters, but it also made for uncomfortable situations. The black firefighters rarely talked to their white colleagues about their monthly B-Force meetings. It made for an awkward atmosphere because many of the black and white guys were very close. Even some of the black firefighters seemed to feel uneasy about the secrecy.

B-Force always bothered me. I used to write "KILL WHITEY" on the notices for B-Force meetings that were posted on the bulletin boards. I did this half-jokingly, but also to make the black firefighters think about the effect that this club had on the white firefighters.

Every new black firefighter was actively recruited to join B-Force and I imagine that the pressure to join was immense. Most of the black firefighters were members, but some of the veterans stayed out. They were not as easily swayed by peer pressure.

One day I was the only white firefighter out of the nine on duty at Station Number One. All of a sudden the black firefighters started filing out of the engine house – for a B-Force meeting. One of the veteran black firefighters said to me, "Hey Mike, I'm gonna stay back and ride with you if we get an alarm." I asked him why he wasn't going to the B-Force meeting and I'll never forget what he said: "I don't support organizations that promote killing whitey." Of course, he was joking. They really didn't talk about killing whitey, or anybody else for that matter. In fact, they did many good things for the community. They sponsored youth sports, mentored young kids, and were active in various other community activities. But the bottom line is that the organization was a conflict of interest and didn't belong in the fire department.

Years ago, when the city and fire department were predominately white, there probably was a need for B-Force. But the times and the city had changed. The citizen population was about ninety-nine percent black. The city government from the mayor, on down, was predominately black. The fire department was about fifty percent black. What had started as an honest effort to ensure equal treatment seemed to turn into a force for preferential treatment.

Case in point: Numerous black firefighters, whom I trusted, told me that the city administration would do whatever it takes, regardless of promotional exam test scores, to make certain that the fire chief is a black man. Case in point number two: In 2004, the city administration had a certified list of new recruits in ranking order from a written examination that had cost the city $30,000. They planned to hire ten firefighter-medics. (This was shortly after the East Cleveland Fire Department had taken over the EMS services in the city. We had added two ambulances and 5,000 additional medical runs and we needed experienced help desperately.) Most of the recruits in the top thirty were white and many had the paramedic certification. But instead of hiring from the certified list, the acting fire chief, who was a black man, somehow talked the mayor into circumventing the normal hiring procedures and hiring ten "professional" (experienced) firefighters. Eight of the ten firefighters hired were black and only two were paramedics. They were brought in at a much higher rate of pay than if they'd been hired, as in past practice, from the certified civil service list. To top it off, the administration was then going to pay for paramedic school for the group. Of the ten "professionals" they hired, seven quit within two years to go to other departments.

One of the most blatant conflicts of interest took place in 2006. The members of B-Force voted to allow the newly appointed fire chief to join their organization. Never before had a non-union member been allowed into B-Force, let alone one who was part of the city administration. I was flabbergasted, as were the rest of the white firefighters. I would have loved to be a fly on the wall during some of those meetings.

B-Force continued to be a thorn in my side, but the older I got, the more I chose my battles. Then, in 2007, B-Force quietly, and unexpectedly, disbanded. I didn't think it would happen during my career, but it did. I honestly believe that this was a good thing, and that the black and white firefighters would get along better now. B-Force did good work in the community and provided fellowship between the black firefighters, but I believe the department, for the greater good, is better off without it.

There was an occasion when two young kids from the neighborhood came into fire station number two to visit. They were brother and sister. The boy was eight years old and his sister was five. Their clothes were tattered, they were dirty and they smelled as if they hadn't bathed in a while. I asked them if they'd eaten lunch yet and they said no. I sat them down at the kitchen table and fed them.

Along with the other on-duty firefighters we asked them some personal questions. We discovered that they both had birthdays recently but received no presents because "mom couldn't afford it." The same was true for Christmas. They also mentioned that they received $5 from mom for getting good report cards, but had to give the money back so mom could buy food. As they talked, they broke our hearts. They were well-mannered, friendly, and full of love. On this particular day, there were five firefighters at the station, two white and three black. We all wanted to help these kids.

Firefighter Bill Adamczak, who is white, drove his personal vehicle to Wal-Mart and spent over $100 on toys. We all chipped in on the cost. It was heartwarming to see their eyes light up when we gave them the toys. Firefighter Robert Benjamin, a black man, took his personal vehicle to a local store and bought both kids some new clothes to wear and some to take home with them. He also took them into the washroom and let them wash up in our sinks. They ended up staying with us for about three hours until we took them home. We talked to their mother, who actually was a pretty good lady but had run into a long streak of bad luck and misfortune. She expressed her appreciation, but just seeing how happy the kids were made it all worthwhile.

There was another incident that was tragic and almost fatal for one of our black firefighters, Jonathan Alexander. On the morning of May 8, 2010, three young thugs broke into Jon's house. According to police, they were looking for drugs but had gotten some bad information on the house where the drugs were supposedly located. Jon left work at 8:30 A.M. and went straight home. When he entered his house and confronted them, one of the three shot him in the back from point-blank range. The bullet struck his colon, small intestine, and pancreas before exiting through his chest. When he arrived at the hospital, he had numbness in both legs and internal bleeding. He was in critical condition and was rushed to surgery.

He needed six units of blood as well as additional plasma. His blood pressure dropped so low that he nearly went into cardiac arrest. Jon almost died but thanks to the tremendous work of the Cleveland EMS crew who treated him in the field and transported him to Huron Hospital, as well as the trauma team of doctors and nurses at Huron, he was stabilized.

When Jon was in surgery, the intensive care waiting room was packed with firefighters, police officers, and city officials alike. They were black, white, young, old, male, and female. There was on-duty, off-duty, and even former East Cleveland firefighters present. Our police department was well represented. The mayor, assistant to the mayor, fire chief, and executive assistant were there. Each and every person in the waiting room took their turn giving Jon's parents a hug, shaking hands with his brothers and friends, and showing their support.

Even though the mood was somber, it made me feel fantastic to see the outpouring of support for a brother firefighter at a very critical time in his life. It told me not only something about the people in the waiting room, but also about Jon Alexander. I already considered Jon to be a great guy and a great firefighter. This scene showed that he was a man who befriended both white and black folks by simply being himself. Fortunately, Jon went on to make an almost full recovery without any paralysis.

The beauty of stories like these is that race was not an issue. It was about people helping people, regardless of differences in skin color.

Dispatcher: "9-1-1, what's your emergency?"

9-1-1 caller: "Um, I'm not sure if this is an emergency but it feels like something is stuck up my vagina!"

(Actual 9-1-1 call)

CHAPTER 11

War Story 3: *Elevator Fatality*

I looked outside of the apparatus bay door to a clear, warm, sunny sky. No chance of rain today. I just knew that this was going to be a great day. Suddenly the alarm bells sounded and I moved toward Engine 114, the apparatus that I was assigned to that day. The call was for a serviceman possibly trapped in an elevator shaft at a high-rise apartment building. I had just over four years on the job then and had never had a call quite like this. I had gone to calls for people stuck inside an elevator, but never for a person trapped in the elevator shaft.

Engine 114 crew arrived at the twenty-six-story high-rise apartment building on Terrace Road in about three minutes. We were informed that a serviceman had been working inside the elevator shaft and when the exterior door to the elevator shut, it caused the car to descend. The serviceman was not responding to calls from the building maintenance personnel.

You can tell a lot about the severity of the situation from body language of people at the scene. Sometimes they are freaking out, other times they have that blank stare of disbelief. Either way, we immediately knew that the end result would probably not be a good one. Someone had failed to follow proper safety procedures. Power to the elevator should have been shut off before the serviceman entered the shaft.

Captain Charlie Catania impressed me by how he took control of this emergency scene. He immediately ordered the maintenance manager to cut the power to all elevators in the building. He asked him where the serviceman was when the car came down. The maintenance manager said that the man had been working in the shaft just below the mezzanine. He said that the last words he heard the serviceman say were, "Oh shit."

By now news reporters and television cameras were on scene, gawking through the first-floor front windows which provided a direct view to the bank of elevators. Captain Catania ordered the property manager to keep them outside and to cover the glass so that the camera people would be unable to film the scene. That was a relief to me because the situation was already quite stressful.

Less than two minutes later, the maintenance manager informed us that the elevators were now disabled. There were no elevator keys on site, and at that time we were operating without a set of elevator door keys on our apparatus. Since time was of the essence and there was a very real possibility of serious danger to the serviceman, Captain Catania ordered us to use the extricating tool known as "the jaws of life" on the door on the ground level. At this point it wasn't really a big issue that we were going to damage these doors.

We had the elevator door forced open in about three minutes. We looked into the shaft, then upward toward the bottom of the elevator car. It was fairly dark and I could only see the steel cables and metal framework that were attached to the elevator car. I did not see a body. We began calling out the serviceman's name, but the silence was deafening.

Suddenly Firefighter Doug Flanders approached Captain Catania and said that he could see a leg hanging down behind a large section of metal about ten feet above ground level. Hearing this, I immediately looked into the dark shaft. At first I didn't see anything other than the stalled car and the metal framework that made up the tracks and access ladders for the cars. Then I saw it, an image that will be etched in my mind forever. The leg was bent in a way that would only be possible if it were severely broken, hanging just below the car with the metal framework blocking the view of the rest of the body. I couldn't even tell whether the leg was still attached.

Flanders climbed up the access ladder inside the shaft, then informed Captain Catania that the man was dead. The force of the car had caused massive internal injuries; he'd had no chance of surviving the impact. We now had the unenviable task of getting this poor guy's body out of the dark, dreary elevator shaft. But there was no easy way to move the body because the car was pinning it against the metal framework.

By now a supervisor from the elevator company was on scene, but he was so upset that he could hardly speak and his hands were trembling uncontrollably. Catania quickly realized that this man would be of no use in his present mental state and told him to go sit down and catch his breath.

Catania ordered everyone out of the elevator shaft and informed maintenance to turn the electrical power back on to the elevators. He then told maintenance to raise the elevator car up about five feet, then shut the power back off.

What happened next is best described as eerie – very, very eerie.

Flanders and I had to enter the cold, dark, creepy shaft and climb up to the limp, mangled body of this man who, thirty minutes earlier had been very much alive. We had to tie a rope around his body, then untangle it from the metal framework. When we finally managed to free him, we lowered the body down to the basement level of the elevator shaft. The entire time, I couldn't help but wonder if the car might somehow fail and come crashing down on us too, resulting in two more fatalities. When I had signed on to be a firefighter, I'd never imagined a scenario like this.

At the bottom of the shaft, we had to put this man into a body bag. This was probably the worst part of the entire scene for me. This guy seemed to be about my age. I imagine he probably had a couple kids. He had gotten up that morning and gone to work, like always, fully expecting to go home that night to his family.

If the power to the elevator had been shut off, this tragedy never would have happened. I found out later that someone had jammed a screwdriver under the elevator door to hold it open while the man worked. Unfortunately, the screwdriver didn't stay in place. The door shut and the car went down, crushing the serviceman to a point where he was asphyxiated.

I had seen dead bodies before this, and saw many more after, but this day was one I'll never forget. I thought about the dark, dreary elevator shaft, wrapping the body in the body bag, the finality of zipping it shut. I realized how precious life really is and how fleeting it can be. On this day I adopted my new life motto: "Every day on the right side of the dirt is a good day."

After being splashed in the mouth with blood from a patient and the patient repeatedly stating that he was okay...

Firefighter to patient:
"I don't care if you're okay. Just tell me that you haven't stuck yourself with needles or fucked any whores lately!"

(Actual EMS run)

CHAPTER 12

Ball Busting

There is a lot of down time in a fire station, and it's only fitting that guys will think of many unusual or quirky things to do to pass the time. This includes having fun at someone else's expense, more commonly known as "ball busting." It's almost like being in a college fraternity house or some kind of club for immature boys. I always thought that there was no future in growing up entirely. I've even told some of the no-nonsense, uptight individuals I've known to "grow down," because they didn't seem to know how to laugh or have a little fun. Hell, life is way too short to be serious all of the time.

New recruits, or "boots," are the top targets for practical jokes. They are such easy marks because they're usually on probation for a year and have to be on their best behavior. Plus, they don't know anything, so they trust guys who have been on the job for a while. It's usually pretty easy to set them up for a nice prank. It's all part of paying your dues and it's usually good-natured.

For example: Firefighter Dennis Dixon told a couple of new recruits that the chief wanted to see them upstairs in his office immediately. When the recruits asked what the chief wanted, Dixon told them he didn't know for sure, but the chief wanted the recruits to report to him in their full turnout gear (bunker pants, coat, hood, helmet, and gloves), including the self-contained breathing apparatus (SCBA), with face pieces on, breathing tank air.

After donning their gear and face pieces, the recruits hustled upstairs and knocked on the chief's door. The chief, who knew nothing about the prank, just stared incredulously at the two rookies standing there in full war gear, breathing tank air from their SCBA's.

"Did you want to see us, Chief?" one of the rookies asked. The chief told them to get the hell out of his office and closed the door in their faces. The recruits were dumbfounded, then finally realized that they'd been set up by Dixon, who was hiding in the adjacent room so he could listen in. He had to struggle to suppress his laughter when the chief closed the door on the rookies. But he said he heard the chief belly laughing in his office. Everybody likes messing with the new meat!

One of the traditional pranks passed on through the years in East Cleveland is telling the boots that they need to check a drain in an outdoor underground water pit in the parking lot during the annual apparatus pump tests. This prank is similar to one that the Cleveland Browns veterans play on their rookies, sending them on a wild goose chase all over town to pick up some non-existent Thanksgiving turkeys.

During our apparatus pump test, we flow water from the fire engine through a hose and out of a large-volume nozzle into an underground holding pit. From this pit we can take water into the engine and also discharge it back into the pit. In this manner, we are able to test the pumping capacity of our trucks without wasting water into a sewer drain.

The boots are told prior to the pump test that the drain in the bottom of the pit needs to be checked before we can proceed. The pit is only accessible through a small rectangular steel lid at the surface, barely bigger than a manhole cover. The pit is about three feet wide and ten feet in length and probably about ten feet deep. It's always full of water and the visibility is zero. This confined space would probably spook a professional diver. And of course, there's no drain.

Before the boots enter the pit, we tell them they must wear the proper protective gear. After all, we are the fire service and safety is our main concern! At our urging, they put on shorts and a t-shirt, a snorkel, face mask, and fins, and in case they run into problems down there, a SCBA.

To be clear, we have no intention of sending the boots down into the pit. It's a test to see how far they will go. They are normally young and dumb, and very eager to impress, so the prank almost always goes as planned.

When they are dressed and ready to enter the pit, we have one of the "divers" sit on the edge of the access hole with their feet dangling into the water. The other divers hold a rescue rope, while donning their own snorkels and face pieces in case they are called into action. By this time, they are sweating bullets – especially the ones who can't swim. Just before the first diver takes the plunge, the cameras come out and we photograph these ridiculous-looking nervous rookies while the veterans burst into laughter. The boots feel foolish, but the relief of not going into the pit eases the pain. New photographs of recruit divers are added to scrapbooks and the boots can't wait until the next class of rookies comes along so they can lead the charge in setting them up for the next diving expedition.

Fire station number one has a cold, dark, narrow tunnel in the basement that we used for storage. The tunnel serves as a pathway for steam and electrical lines and if you follow it to the end, you wind up almost directly underneath the adjoining city jail. When we were really bored we liked to taunt the prisoners and throw firecrackers near the cracks and crevices in the cell walls. But the best tunnel prank involves a Halloween mask.

Many have fallen prey to this prank, one in particular became famous. During the morning and afternoon hours, the senior firefighters set him up with wild stories about an escaped prisoner. They even got a police officer to come to the fire station and warn everyone that an extremely dangerous murderer had escaped from the jail and was most likely hiding out in the vicinity. The seed was now planted in the victim's head and the prank was set in motion.

Later on that evening, a senior firefighter sneaked down to the tunnel with a mask. Then one of the shift lieutenants told the recruit to go down into the tunnel and get a case of toilet paper. The recruit reluctantly complied. After all, what could he say? He was a new boot and he had no choice but to go down into the tunnel and complete this important detail. As soon as he descended the basement steps, all of the remaining firefighters stationed themselves near the top of the steps to witness his reaction. He turned left near the supply cage then made his way to the cheap wooden door that accessed the tunnel.

The firefighter who was hiding in the tunnel had previously unscrewed all but one light bulb to make the tunnel even darker than it normally was. As the recruit reached for the case of toilet paper, the masked "killer" jumped out and let out a muffled grunt as he rushed toward him. The recruit screamed, turned and bolted for the basement steps. But when he got to the steps, he was so scared that he couldn't climb them. His legs and body were so out of sync that he was basically cavitating like a car in neutral whose driver is hammering the gas pedal. Instead of climbing the steps, he just kept knocking his knees and shins against them.

By this time, the firefighters at the top of the steps and the masked man in the tunnel were crying with laughter. The recruit firefighter finally realized that the joke was on him and he tried to gather himself. When he finally settled down after about a half an hour, he admitted that he'd almost pissed himself. He was a pretty good sport about the whole thing, especially considering the cuts on his legs.

The deputy chief was upset because the horseplay had resulted in an injury. But while I'll never know for sure, I can't help but to believe that as soon as the deputy chief chewed out the men for the prank, he went back into his office and had a good laugh!

We also used the scary mask in a supply closet with excellent results, aside from the time it backfired on me. Firefighter Rick Wilcox and I set up Cornell "Catfish" Penland, who was fairly new at the time. When Penland opened the door to get supplies I stuck my head out and scared the shit out of him, but he slammed the door right in my face and damn near knocked me out. It hurt like hell but there was no way I could get mad because I was the one who started the prank. In the end we all had a really good laugh.

The dormitory was a prime location for pranks. One popular joke involved removing the supports to the bed frame so that when the victim gets in the bed it falls right to the floor with a loud bang. Another involves rigging a CO_2 fire extinguisher so that when the victim gets in bed the extinguisher discharges. Of course, there is the old favorite "short sheeting," folding the top sheet in half so that when the victim tries to get into the bed he can't stretch out his legs.

Another fire department favorite is freezing a saline water IV bag, then strategically mounting it on the ceiling above the victim's bed with the plastic tubing pointed down. The goal of the prank is for the victim to dream he is being subjected to the "Chinese water torture." Timing and stealth are crucial in this prank because you don't want the victim to notice the bag and you want the water to melt when the lights are out and the victim is sleeping. This joke is hilarious when it's pulled off successfully, but it is one of the more difficult ones to master.

Fire department practical jokes are a part of almost all departments and are normally pretty harmless. Some people handle the jokes better than others and eventually you learn who can take it and who cannot. The one thing that you need to learn quickly in this business is that you can't have thin skin because the chances are, if you do, you will be abused more because of the entertainment value that you provide to the practical jokers.

> *9-1-1 caller: "I need an ambulance cause my hands are super-glued together."*
>
> *Dispatcher: "How are you holding the phone then?"*
>
> *(Actual 9-1-1 call)*

CHAPTER 13

Real Heroes… or Not?

After the 9/11 World Trade Center attacks, there was a public perception that all firefighters are heroes. To put it bluntly, that's bullshit. Being a hero is like gaining respect — it doesn't come automatically. It is earned. This doesn't mean that firefighters aren't brave, courageous people, because, for the most part, they are. But there is a difference between doing your job and doing something heroic in the line of duty. Many firefighters will never be called on to do something heroic. Heroism is achieved by going above and beyond the call of duty, or putting yourself in harm's way to help a fellow human being.

We rescued an unconscious man who was lying on a smoky bedroom floor during a fire at a high-rise apartment building. There was a very good chance that he would have died had we not found him. It would have been easy to call those involved with the rescue heroes, and not get too much argument to the contrary. But the fact of the matter is that this man was saved by a well-executed search, rescue, and fire attack. There was enough smoke in the apartment to kill this man but the fire was small and the heat intensity was low. We did our jobs. No heroism was required. It is a tremendous feeling to know that you helped save someone's life, but the fact remains that heroism is a label that belongs only on true heroes, no exceptions!

In my opinion, the real heroes are the men and women in the armed forces. They are the people who are dodging bullets and bombs on a daily basis, fighting for the freedom of all Americans. They are the ones who have to kill others in order for people like me to enjoy freedom. I was once told by a Vietnam veteran that life is never the same after you take another man's life from him. I felt bad for him and at the same time felt lucky that I was never put in that position. I would have done so, if called upon, but I just missed the draft at the end of the Vietnam war and was too old when Desert Storm took place.

I can only imagine the horror of war. My heart goes out to all soldiers and their families and I will never be able to express my undying gratitude for the sacrifice that these true heroes have made, and still make, for our freedom. They are what make the United States the greatest country on the planet.

There are other heroes, too. There are policemen, firefighters, EMS workers, and many others who have done heroic deeds. But there needs to be an opportunity for a person to be a hero. There are some damn good firefighters who probably would've been heroes if they'd had the opportunity.

There is a fine line, however, between being heroic and being foolish. Firefighters have standard operating procedures (S.O.P.s) that they are supposed to follow. These S.O.P.'s are based on the best tactical ways to operate in a safe manner at the emergency scene and successfully complete the task at hand. S.O.P.'s are tactics and strategies devised from a collection of data and opinions from reliable text books and knowledgeable, as well as experienced veteran firefighters and officers. Firefighters study and train on S.O.P.'s in order to become proficient at their job. But sometimes at the emergency scene, the shit hits the fan. Unexpected things happen, danger increases, the scene gets intense, and the adrenaline flows like hot lava. These are the times when S.O.P.'s get changed on the fly or, at times, get tossed out altogether. Two incidents come to mind.

An East Ohio Gas Company serviceman called on us to rescue two of his fellow service workers who had been overcome by natural gas fumes. They reportedly were lying unconscious at the bottom of a manhole. ECFD responded and arrived on scene to find, sure enough, two workers unconscious and lying face down in about four inches of water. There was a loud hissing sound as natural gas rushed from a hole in the two-inch supply pipe that the servicemen had been attempting to repair.

We call an incident like this a confined space rescue. Such incidents are rare, and in East Cleveland, the firefighters receive only minimal training for them. This type of rescue is best performed by tactical rescue teams that specialize and train regularly. But when you get to the emergency scene and see two unconscious men in a hole in a do-or-die situation, you do the best you can and hope that things work out.

Engine 114 and Truck 121 responded to this incident with two four-man crews. The confined space rescue equipment that we had was kept on Ladder Truck 121. The S.O.P. called for setting up the tripod, rescue ropes, and other specialized equipment. But time was of the essence and this would have taken too long, considering our unfamiliarity with the equipment. Firefighter Jerry Jones immediately grabbed a 14-foot straight metal ladder from Engine 114 and lowered it into the manhole. He then donned his SCBA and masked up.

Without regard for his own safety, Jones climbed down into the hole. A rescue rope was lowered into the hole and, one at a time, Jones secured the rope around the men and steadied them as the firefighters above pulled the unconscious men from the manhole. The two men were taken to the hospital and made a full recovery.

Sparks from the ladder or the SCBA could have caused an explosion that would have killed about ten people. Jones received heroism awards from Firehouse magazine and the firefighter's union, Local 500. He also received oral reprimands for not following departmental S.O.P.'s. and putting himself and his co-workers in danger.

Was Jones a hero or just reckless? That's an easy answer for me: On that day, Firefighter Jones was a true hero. Two men are alive because of his courage and fast action. Not everyone would have had the stones to go into that manhole under those circumstances.

Others would say that Jones was reckless, and there are strong arguments for that view too. But I believe that if our protocol had been followed that day, those two East Ohio Gas company employees would be dead. I'll take that trade-off. As Jones likes to say, "It is what it is."

The other incident that comes to mind was a call to rescue a man down in an underground electrical vault. This vault was a narrow, shallow space that was accessed through a manhole and was located four feet under the middle of a busy main street named Superior Avenue. The vault contained extremely high-voltage electrical lines and transformers. Service technicians, this time from the Cleveland Electric Illuminating Company, had committed a cardinal sin in safety by not making sure that the power to the vault was locked out before they entered the space.

On this day I was in charge of Engine 111 crew, a newly appointed lieutenant with less than a year of experience as an officer. Our crew was on a detail at the time that the call came over the radio, and as soon as I heard it I knew that this did not sound good. I was almost relieved because, due to our location, we would not be the first arriving apparatus. Usually we want to be "first in" at an emergency scene. But, honestly, on this occasion, I was glad that we were not. And when we finally arrived, right after Truck 121 and Engine 114, I was stunned by what I saw.

Twenty-year veteran firefighter Jeff Polson had entered the manhole and was standing there preparing to lift a victim out and into the street. The victim was lying face down, motionless on the concrete floor inside the vault. Every instinct in my body told me that this was completely wrong and extremely dangerous. However, it was too late because rescue was in progress. Polson was a very good friend of mine and a man that I looked up to. He had more experience than me and I felt a bit awkward telling him what to do. I always thought, and still do, that he should've been promoted long before me, but that's another story. I could only watch in horror as he lifted the man from the ground and up to the opening in the manhole, scared shitless that my buddy was going to suffer the same fate as the victim who he was lifting out of the hole.

But Polson got the man and himself out safely. The paramedics immediately started working on the lifeless victim in the middle of Superior Avenue. His co-worker's face was as white as a ghost. At first he had been unable to answer our questions as to whether the power to the vault had been locked out, but we eventually ascertained that the vault was hot. The victim had bumped up against some extremely high-voltage electrical lines and was probably killed instantly by more than 10,000 volts.

My pal Jeff could have very easily suffered the same fate. He put himself in harm's way in order to try to save a fellow man. Just as it was with Firefighter Jones, and contrary to some Monday morning quarterbacks, I call this man a hero. The outcome was different in this incident — it ended up being a body recovery, but we didn't know that upon arrival. Jeff did what many people would not have had the courage to do. I commend him for his bravery. And I would have missed drinking beer with him and kicking his ass on the golf course!

I learned so much from these two incidents. I witnessed courage that I'd never seen before. I felt the intensity, the tension and the adrenaline rush. I learned that as a line officer I will sometimes be put in a position to make decisions that will affect the well-being of citizens as well as other men in my crew. I realized that we don't train enough. I learned that we are not always going to be prepared for every situation and that we may need to improvise occasionally. Most importantly, I learned that we need to share these experiences with others in order to get better.

I decided that day that if we ever had another situation like those two incidents and I was making the decisions, my first concern would always be for the safety of my firefighters. No firefighter in my crew would ever be allowed to enter any confined space or other hazardous environment where there is imminent danger and it may be a body recovery. This may sound callous, but if victims die because of these decisions, so be it. When people ask what our job is, the standard reply has always been "to save lives and property." The real answer is "to assure the safety of firefighters, then save lives and property." I'm going to make sure that my brother and sister firefighters all go home to our families.

Dispatcher: "9-1-1, what's your emergency"?

9-1-1 caller: "There's a huge fire across from 14015".

Dispatcher: "14015 what"?

9-1-1 caller: East Cleveland motherfucker"!

CHAPTER 14

Perimeter Man

Without question, the single most insulting label for a firefighter in East Cleveland was "Perimeter Man."

Perimeter Man is sluggish, hesitant, and slow to get inside a burning building to join his comrades in the fire attack. Perimeter Man prefers the clean, fresh outside air to the toxic black smoky air inside the burning building. He can't see a hard charging firefighter inside a burning building because he is in the middle of the heat and smoke, in zero visibility. You can't see the Perimeter Man inside of the burning building either, because he isn't there. He's hiding in the backyard, behind a fire truck, on the stairwell landing, or in the basement.

When the hard charging interior firefighter is called upon to attack the fire, he does so in a swift, aggressive, deliberate manner, knowing that time is of the essence and his effort could determine whether they are working the fire for one hour or four. Perimeter Man, meanwhile, tries his best to find a job that takes him as far from the danger as possible.

Perimeter Man is well versed in slowly shutting down the utilities even when there is no smoke or fire in a basement. He will gladly perform this job and will take twice as long as it requires. He is quick to offer his services to throw a ground ladder up to ventilate the exterior windows instead of taking a hose line inside. He will gladly assist the fire truck drivers with the hookup of water supply lines. Simply put, the Perimeter Man is a firefighter who has managed to slip through the cracks to get the job but is not suited for the work. As far as I know, the name was coined in East Cleveland.

There are two types of Perimeter Men. Some guys are just flat-out lazy and attempt to stay away from the interior fire operations because that is where the bulk of the grunt work is performed. He is not really afraid to go inside, he just doesn't like to get his hands dirty. He may also be considered to be a "Prima Donna." He will do everything he can to get out of work while his co-workers are busting their tails. He doesn't feel guilty about this either. This type of Perimeter Man is almost always a veteran firefighter, because a new man would not be able to get away with this type of behavior. (In the Akron Fire Department, they refer to this type of firefighter simply as a "slug.")

Some of the veteran Perimeter Men were not always that way, but they got old and fat and lost their edge. These guys will usually make it to retirement but will be less respected than the guys who worked hard their entire careers.

The second type of Perimeter Man is worse than the first. This is a guy who has always had reservations about going inside a fire or who has had his edge compromised in the past, resulting in apprehension. If a guy knows that he is afraid to go inside a fire, then he should resign from the fire service immediately, plain and simple. Fighting fires is not for everybody! This is something he will know after his first few fires. I am really not sure why this type of Perimeter Man stays in the fire service. He understands that what he is doing is dangerous. Subconsciously he knows that he is scared to death inside a burning building, but he is in denial about his shortcomings. It's possible he believes that he will eventually overcome his fears and go into a fire with the aggression and confidence that he sees in his fellow firefighters. But that's rare. Most guys with apprehensions will never get over them. Some will leave the profession, but others will stay and attempt to "fake the funk," as the saying goes.

I recall three Perimeter Men in particular from my years in the department. One was an officer when I began, so I don't really know whether he was always like that or if he'd lost his edge at some point. Probably the latter, because some of the older firefighters didn't view him as a Perimeter Man. But it became apparent to me after a few years on the job that this officer wasn't a hard charger. I know of no other officer or firefighter who was able to "fake the funk" longer than this guy. He was famous for telling his crew that the fire was "down the hallway, to the left." This meant that he was not going to be joining them on the attack line, which was contrary to our standard operating procedures. An officer is supposed to be positioned directly behind the nozzle man and in front of the backup man.

I once saw him remain on the top step of a hallway while the two other firefighters in his crew advanced a hose line through the thick smoke and heat without him. I had to step around him to perform my assignment of ventilating the interior windows. He was later called out on this but was protected by the O.I.C. and was not disciplined.

The two other Perimeter Men I knew were very apprehensive during firefighting. It was said by many firefighters and officers that when the bells went off, these guys started having anxiety attacks. This can get people hurt. A weak link in the platoon jeopardizes everyone's safety.

One of these guys was driving a pumper to a confirmed working fire when I was the lieutenant in charge of the truck. He was driving so slowly that I asked him what the hell he was doing. His face was so flustered from the anxiety setting in that I wondered if we would make it to the scene safely.

The other guy always managed to find jobs other than fire attack to avoid going inside. Both of these guys were not suited for the fire service. They were also a detriment to the department inside the engine house. Thankfully they were both gone with less than eight years on the job, and we were much better off without them.

Perimeter Men can only fly under the radar for so long. Most either leave on their own or are forced out. If a new guy admits that he is not comfortable going inside a burning building, then decides to pursue another occupation, he is respected much more than the guy who stays on and pretends.

Dispatcher: "Why can't you walk, sir?"

9-1-1 caller: "Cause my feet be puffy!"

(Actual 9-1-1 call)

CHAPTER 15

War Story 4: The Ultimate Paradise

It was a sunny fall Saturday afternoon in 1992. I was approaching my five-year anniversary date with the fire department. My cousin John Hart, former East Cleveland firefighter, had told me that time would fly on this job, and I was starting to believe him. He also told me that I will see more in my first five years working in East Cleveland than many firefighters will see in an entire career. On this day I saw something that, prior to then, I'd only seen in the movies.

The call came in on the 911 line as a domestic quarrel that had resulted in a shooting, with multiple victims. This incident occurred before our department had taken over control of the EMS service for the city. We were, however, available to assist the ambulances and go out as first responders in the fire apparatus, if needed. On this day there were two ambulances on scene with a call in for a third and Engine 114 from our fire station. I was driving Engine 114 and part of a four-man crew.

We responded north on Doan Avenue to a cluster of three-story apartment buildings. The only information we had was that they needed additional manpower to help stabilize, package, and transport patients. Upon our arrival we still did not know how many victims there were or what their condition was. I pulled Engine 114 to the side of the road and parked behind the ambulances. My lieutenant and two crew members got out and proceeded into the apartment building. Since I was the driver, I elected to stay with my apparatus unless I was needed inside.

As I sat there in Engine 114, I looked around. There were at least five police cars, a couple of unmarked detective cars, two ambulances and our fire truck. At that time, I really hadn't seen a whole lot of blood and guts. That was about to change. My lieutenant came out of the building, walked up to Engine 114, and said "Hey Ede, you gotta come in here and see this shit, you won't believe it."

We entered the front door and started up the stairs to the second floor. As I stepped onto the second-floor landing area, my eyes were fixed to the floor, particularly to the right side, where a heavy blood trail ran from the apartment door in front of me to the stairs going to the third floor.

I walked into the apartment and tiptoed around the blood that was all over the floor. Five feet from the door was a blood-soaked rifle lying on the floor. To my right was a detective and a uniformed police officer. Everyone seemed to be very calm, but my heart was pounding. What I saw next was a sight that I'll always remember. I looked to my left and saw a middle-aged black man slumped down in a chair. His head was tilted to the left, exposing a large bullet hole in the right side of his neck. Blood from this wound almost entirely drenched his white t-shirt and extended onto his pants and down to the chair and floor. He looked to be about 35 to 40 years old, somewhat tall and lanky. His eyes were wide open, but lifeless. I stared at the hole in his neck for a few seconds. I thought about how quickly life can be taken away from you and how this man had no idea when he woke up that morning that he would suffer this fate while watching football and drinking beer with friends.

The detective informed us that there had been a lot of drinking going on, which led to an argument, then fist fighting, and eventually escalated into the shootings. He told us that there were three people involved in the altercation and all three had been shot. The guy in the chair in front of me was obviously dead. Looking around, I saw no other bodies and there were no EMS personnel in this suite. Just then, my lieutenant waved for me to come out into the hallway.

We proceeded up the stairs to the third floor, following a very distinct blood trail that led into the first apartment on the left. As soon as the door was opened I saw a middle-aged black female on the cot being attended to by two paramedics. She had a white gauze bandage wrapped around her head. The gauze was blood-soaked on the left side where a bullet had struck the side of her skull. She was unconscious and barely breathing. The medics had already inserted a breathing tube in her and started to administer oxygen and drugs. They transported her to Huron Hospital, and I found out later that she had died shortly after arriving.

At this point, I had seen enough. There was another victim who was in the same third-floor suite who had been shot, but not fatally. I really didn't have a desire to gawk anymore because, realistically, that was what we were doing. The paramedics had everything under control.

Afterwards, I didn't get queasy or sick to my stomach. I also wasn't really affected psychologically, probably because I didn't know the victims. Still, this was a very powerful and eye-opening experience. I felt bad for the victims, but I also felt a bit angry at the senselessness of it all. Here we had three people who knew each other, watching football together on a Saturday afternoon. The scene turned ugly and two of the three were dead. For what?

I never did get all of the details as to exactly what happened, nor did I attempt to. Even if I found out the details, they would never have made sense to me. I was glad that it didn't affect me mentally because I knew that this would not be the last time for blood, guts, and dead bodies on the job. I knew that, in order to perform my job as best as I could, I would need to eliminate any personal feelings for victims at the emergency scene. I also realized that I was glad to be a firefighter instead of a cop or paramedic. I take my hat off to the men and women in those professions because they really earn their money. I knew at that time that I'd rather run into a burning building than dodge bullets or deal with the blood and guts on a regular basis.

The gruesome scene that I saw that day on Doan Avenue would be one of many that I would see through the course of my career. The harsh reality of it was that this city where I worked was very violent and murders happened far too frequently. I will never forget the ride back to the fire station from this incident. We passed a street sign that declared "East Cleveland, the Ultimate Paradise." I thought to myself, "Ya Right!"

Retired East Cleveland Firefighter Jeff Polson: "We used to hire firefighters who read pussy magazines. Now we hire pussies who read firefighter magazines!"

CHAPTER 16

Squad Knobs

When I became a firefighter in 1988, EMS – Emergency Medical Service – was only a small part of our duties. In my mind I had signed on to be a firefighter only and I wanted no part of any EMS duties. All firefighters were required to be basic Emergency Medical Technicians, but we rarely responded to EMS emergencies. The advanced life-support EMS duties for the city were provided by Huron Hospital until 2001. The ambulances were kept at the hospital and they responded to calls from there. Every once in a while, they would call on us to assist with a large patient or to go as a first responder when they were unavailable. But they handled the lion's share of EMS emergencies by themselves.

Of the 53 firefighters on the department roster in 1988, only one was certified as a paramedic. Because we had so few EMS runs our skill level suffered and, collectively, the level of care that we could provide was not very good. It was a terrible feeling when responding to an EMS emergency with a fire truck, knowing that all four guys aboard were not very good basic EMTs. Even worse, we could not transport patients in the truck. All we could do was provide basic life support and wait for the ambulance. We always hoped that the calls were not too serious and, most of the time, they weren't. However, there were a few times when we felt helpless during actual life-threatening medical emergencies.

There was one incident, in particular, that I will always remember. It was a call for an infant not breathing (my worst nightmare!). It was early morning, around 9 A.M. All of the ambulances were tied up on calls, which was very unusual, especially for this time of the day. At the time I had only been on the job for two to three years and had experienced only a handful of EMS runs. I was fresh out of EMT school so I was familiar with CPR, probably more so than the veteran firefighters and officer who responded with me. But I had never performed CPR on a human being, so to say I was nervous would be an understatement.

We arrived on scene and noticed one police cruiser parked directly in front of a single-family house. When we walked into the living room, the police officers were doing their best to administer CPR to the limp, lifeless body of the tiny infant. They hurriedly passed the child off to the veteran firefighters who had walked in the door ahead of me. The veteran firefighters continued on with CPR, but to no avail. The child was not responding.

I was only a spectator at this call, but the feeling of helplessness was overwhelming for all safety force personnel present. The child's mother, however, seemed almost unaffected, showing none of the emotions you might expect in a crisis like this. After a couple minutes we considered breaking the transport rule and taking the infant to the hospital in the fire truck, but then word came over the radio that an ambulance was on the way.

Four or five minutes later, the ambulance arrived and the two paramedics took over and almost immediately transported the still-lifeless infant to Huron Hospital. Later we learned that the child was pronounced dead in the emergency room, and that the mother was a crack cocaine addict, which explained her lack of emotion at the scene. The infant had been born addicted to crack.

Chances are, this child probably wouldn't have lived even if an advanced life-support ambulance had arrived first on scene. It was very frustrating, nevertheless. It was frustrating because the poor infant child didn't ask to be born a crack addict. It was frustrating that the ambulance was not available when the call came in. And it was frustrating that we were not better equipped and trained to respond to EMS emergencies. We were behind the times. Most departments had already made the transition to also functioning as paramedics, but we were holding out and, to be honest with you, I wanted to specialize as a firefighter for my entire career, if possible.

This all took place in 1991. It would be ten more years until the Huron Hospital big wigs finally decided that they were finished with the ambulance service based out of their hospital. They had the leverage to force our hand and we had no choice but to take on the EMS service and 5,000 annual EMS emergency runs. We added two ambulances to our fleet of fire trucks. The real "kick in the nuts" was that we were only paid two annual $2,000 lump-sum payments for taking on those 5,000 runs. Our base pay rate didn't increase, and it was already among the lowest in the state. That was a hell of a workload increase that didn't go away after two years and two payments.

So, in the year 2001, much to the chagrin of the firefighters, the East Cleveland Fire Department finally began the transition into the world of EMS. The younger firefighters, who were going to be doing most of the work on the ambulances, were soon christened with a new nickname.

All firefighters who were assigned to the ambulances, or "squads," were now called "squad knobs."

"Squad knob" was not a term of endearment. It was an old firefighter slur toward the supposedly inferior EMTs and paramedics who manned the ambulances. I must admit that I was guilty of looking down a bit on EMS guys. But now after seeing them work, I am a bit ashamed of it because these men and women continue to impress me on a regular basis. Squad knob is now a term of respect for those who, day in and day out, get on those "devil busses" and work their tails off, sometimes running 20-25 sleepless calls in a single 24-hour shift.

In the State of Ohio, you must first be certified as an EMT before you can become a paramedic. To obtain both certifications is no easy task. The EMT course lasts about five months and the paramedic course almost a year. Both courses are very intense and involve many hours spent in the classroom. There are also clinical hours at hospitals, hands-on drills, as well as ride time on fire department EMS squads. The tests are rigorous and the training is comprehensive, requiring serious commitment, especially if you work in East Cleveland. Most fire departments pay the $5,000 fee for the class and will detail men on shift to attend classes and pay them overtime on their off days to attend. But not in East Cleveland. Our firefighters were required to pay for the paramedic class out of their own pockets. I always thought that the city's stance on that policy was borderline ridiculous. Yes, the bar is raised high in order to end up with skilled, knowledgeable people, and many do not make the grade. In fact, it is common for students from every EMT and paramedic class to quit or flunk out. The process almost assures that most of the men and women who end up getting certified will be able to perform the job well as they gain experience.

It is now a requirement of most fire departments that those who sit for an entrance examination must be certified as an EMT and paramedic. Other departments who don't have this prerequisite might require new recruits to become EMTs and paramedics within a few years after being hired. And if they don't pass the tests they lose their jobs, plain and simple. Some departments, such as Akron's, will add bonus points to the raw test scores for those who are EMTs or paramedics, giving them a huge advantage over other applicants without those certifications. When there are 3,000 people taking a test for 40-60 positions, it just makes good sense to get certified prior to testing.

Squad knobs earn their money, especially in East Cleveland, where their base salaries are at least $20,000 less than the surrounding communities. They also respond to a significantly higher number of EMS runs, and with only two people, unlike most other communities who staff their ambulances with three and sometimes four people, mostly paramedics. The EMS transition is still a work in progress, as far as getting the entire department to the paramedic level. It will happen eventually, as all new hires are now required to become paramedics within two years.

The East Cleveland squad knobs are truly a rare breed, to say the least. They pretty much had an ambulance service shoved down their throats in 2001 when the department was in no position to take on such a massive responsibility. There were only a handful of paramedics in the department and the EMTs were all inexperienced. I envisioned so many problems with patient care and the operations of the service. But those guys proved me wrong! Talk about stepping up to an enormous challenge and handling it like true champions.

Sure, there were some rough times, especially for our new paramedics. As soon as a guy finished paramedic school, he would get "thrown to the wolves" and start functioning as a medic without the luxury of another experienced paramedic training him for a few months. I remember when Dave Grice, who is truly one of the nicest guys that I have ever met, was so stressed out after becoming a paramedic that I thought he might have a nervous breakdown. There was no orientation or training period for him. He was put into the squad knob rotation immediately after getting certified as a paramedic and was expected to perform advanced life-support techniques on living human beings now without any guidance! Talk about pressure!

Dave, and other guys like him, got through it without suffering any nervous breakdowns. I realize that things aren't always as bad as they seem, but I felt for these guys. They really cared about people and wanted to be able to perform their jobs at a peak level, but to throw them out there like that was just wrong. I commend them all for the fantastic job they did during those first few years.

Once in a while people called the fire station to complain about our squad knobs. Most of the time it was something relating to them having "an attitude" or not providing adequate care to a patient. Most of the time these complaints were unfounded and didn't always tell the entire story.

I received a complaint one day about a couple of our knobs who supposedly wouldn't help a lady with back pain to the ambulance. The caller stated that the patient was his wife and when he looked out the window he saw our guys just standing next to the ambulance, not assisting the patient at all as she walked alone to the ambulance. He said he then went outside to ask why our guys weren't helping his wife. He mentioned that he had a shouting match with one of our knobs and that the knob told him to step back or he was going to call East Cleveland Police. He finished his complaint by telling me that he didn't want to get anyone fired, but thought that our guys needed to be more sensitive to the needs of the patients. I assured him that I would look into the complaint and handle it accordingly.

I looked up the run report in our computer data base to ascertain who had responded to the call and what had transpired. Sure enough, there was more to this story. In the run report narrative, our knobs explained that the man who complained was drunk and belligerent. He said that the patient was able to walk with assistance to the ambulance and that they did, in fact, assist her all the way from inside the house into the ambulance. He said the guy was pissed off because he thought she needed to be on the cot and wheeled to the ambulance, which she really did not. When the guy approached the knobs, he was so threatening that, they told me, they thought they were going to have to fight him. The topper was that the lady with the back pain informed them on the way to the hospital that she initially injured her back due to physical abuse from her husband, the complainant.

That goes to show that there are always two sides to the story and most of the time our guys are vindicated. These squad knobs genuinely care for people and they will almost always go above and beyond the call of duty to make a patient comfortable by providing the best care that they possibly can.

The knobs don't mind the real serious EMS runs like the shootings, stabbings, vehicle accidents, and cardiac arrests. But the ones that drive them crazy and do stir up some attitude in them are the bullshit calls. I can understand how a guy who has been responding to EMS calls for 18 hours straight gets a little bent out of shape when a call for a "headache" or "toe pain" comes in at 3 A.M. It's hard to walk into a residence with a warm smile in a situation like that.

I took a call once from a 17-year-old female who stated that she needed an ambulance because she got a birth control pill stuck in her throat. It was hard for me to hold back my disdain toward her as I asked her if she had tried drinking some water. I told her to drink some water and wait ten minutes, then call back if the pill didn't dissolve. Needless to say, she didn't call back. We are an emergency service but some people think they can call for an ambulance for any minor annoyance.

Another thorn in our side is getting dispatched to the East Cleveland jail, which is the building next door to fire station Number One. It is a very small jail and the cells are on both sides of the walkway. The cells are dark and run-down, and there always seemed to be a foul odor in there. When you pass through the walkway, all eyes are upon you, from cells to the left and right. It's just plain creepy in there!

I've only been in there a couple of times and I hated it. The tension was so thick you could cut it with a knife and I couldn't wait to get the hell out. Most of the calls from the jails are related to prisoners who fake an illness or injury just to get out of their cells. The prisoners are evaluated, treated, and signed off, usually remaining in their cells. I remember when former East Cleveland Firefighter/Medic Mike Hill gave a prisoner an ice pack then told him to sign for it. He was actually signing a refusal of transport form. The prisoner was faking and didn't need to be transported. In hindsight that was pretty funny.

Squad knobs respond to a large number of shootings, stabbings, and assaults. These guys are able to shift into a higher gear when responding to these type of emergencies. I love to watch them work during these high-stress situations. You can tell a lot about a person in this environment. You will see guys who are very confident and cool as a cucumber, and some who are loud, fired up, and anxious. You will also see guys who are tentative, unsure of themselves, who hang in the background while others handle most of the critical care. After the knobs have worked together for a while, they get to understand each other's level of expertise and realize what everyone is best suited to do. It is at this point where they really shine.

They will take a shooting victim laying on the ground in a dangerous environment, and in minutes, have them in the back of the ambulance stabilized with the wounds exposed, a breathing tube in their throat assisted by oxygen, large-bore intravenous lines in place delivering medications, and the patient attached to a heart monitor. Soon after that they will be on their way to the hospital. It is their teamwork and professionalism under duress and adverse conditions that impressed me the most.

These men, our beloved squad knobs, are overworked and underpaid. There are many days when they got little or no sleep in a 24-hour shift. The mental exhaustion is many times worse than the physical exhaustion due to the potential exposure risks, liabilities, and consequences that they face on a daily basis. They have been spat on, bled on, vomited on, pissed on, and even shit on (indirectly). They are exposed to AIDS, hepatitis, meningitis, and other diseases. They frequently encounter drunk or combative patients with whom they have to wrestle or call for police assistance in order to restrain them so they can care for their injuries or illnesses. They are subjected to citizen complaints, court actions, and lawsuits. They respond in ambulances to join the other firefighters to battle working fires when they occur, and after the fire they go right back on the ambulance to finish their shift. They have been called on to respond to EMS calls directly from fire scenes, in their wet, smelly, carcinogen-laden bunker gear. They do this day in and day out.

I salute the squad knobs of East Cleveland. I respect the hell out of them for their hard work. I tell the young guys to be patient because it is at least a twenty-five-year career and eventually they won't have to ride the "devil bus," as former East Cleveland firefighter Severen Henderson used to call it. I do understand, however, that time goes slower when you're a squad knob, especially in the city of East Cleveland, where parallel lines sometimes seem to intersect!

Dispatcher: "9-1-1, what's your emergency?"

911 Caller: "My girlfriend's butt hurts."

CHAPTER 17

Fire Boss

In 2001, I was promoted to the rank of Lieutenant. I had spent the first 13 years of my career as a firefighter. I will always be proud that I was an East Cleveland firefighter. Firefighters are the life blood of the department. They are the glue that holds the department together. I promised myself that if, and when, I became an officer, I would never forget where I came from. I would always support and appreciate the firefighters. I understood that the most difficult scenarios that we face at the emergency scene are best handled by getting input from firefighters. Their experience is invaluable and every officer is better off if they have firefighters sharing information instead of suppressing it. It is a mistake for an officer to micro-manage firefighters. Firefighters make officers look good, and they can also make them look bad. I was not going be an officer who didn't have the trust of the firefighters. That trust was absolutely crucial for an officer to be a competent leader.

The experience gained as a firefighter was essential and I was completely confident that I was more than ready to take the next step as an officer. I learned the job from a long line of aggressive, quick thinking, tradition rich, brave firefighters and officers. East Cleveland firefighters and officers such as Russ Hauser, Jeff Polson, Charlie Catania, Rod Hairston, Jerry Kirchner, Mike Thomas, Rich Kaleal, Al Cellars, Mike Gunn, Dale Hoynacke, Tony Holley, and Tom Flowers, to name a few. There were others too from different shifts than mine. I consider myself extremely lucky to have learned my trade from these fine men.

I embraced the role of Fire Lieutenant. As a Lieutenant, I was responsible for the other three firefighters on my engine or truck company. At this time, a company was comprised of a driver, an officer, and two firefighters. My job at the fire scene was to locate the fire, determine the best way to attack it, and to keep my crew safe in doing so. I was no longer just responsible for myself. I had three others to think about, as well as the added responsibility of making on-the-spot decisions at the fire ground, rescues, and other emergency scenes.

The physical workload for a lieutenant is less than that of a firefighter. The pay rate is obviously higher. It sounds like a pretty good deal, more pay but less work! It is at this point in your career when the job changes significantly. As a lieutenant, you are now called on to use your mind more than your body. The mental part of the job is now at the forefront. With the added responsibility comes added pressure. If you make a mistake now, it could affect three other people, too. Worse yet, if you make a critical tactical error you can get three people, including yourself, badly injured or killed. That is a big part of the tradeoff for less physical work but more pay.

I worked as a lieutenant from 2001-2006. I considered myself a "working officer" because I would frequently help the firefighters pull ceiling and open up walls during working fires. Since we were such a small department, I thought it was necessary to give the men a breather whenever possible. More importantly, I realized that a good officer never forgets where he came from. I always proudly considered myself a firefighter no matter what rank I attained because it's the firefighters who do the real work and make the officers look good. You are only as good as the men who you work with. There are far too many times when an individual is promoted and he lets his ego get in the way of clear thinking. He forgets where he came from and misuses his new-found authority as an officer. He forgets where he came from and, as a result, will end up having problems with some of the firefighters whom he used to work side by side with. The hope is that he comes to his senses and loses the ego. It is crucial that firefighters and officers work together as a team in order to get the best effort from everyone involved.

I was promoted to an Acting Captain's slot in July 2006 due to a shortage of officers at that rank. In East Cleveland the rules permit us to serve as an acting officer for a six-month rotating basis until a promotional test is given to fill the vacancies with permanent officers. You can only function as the O.I.C. (Officer in Command) if you are either a Captain or a Deputy Chief. The O.I.C. is the "Fire Boss" and assumes command of the entire platoon at the emergency scene. As an Acting Captain, I was initially put into this position only when the Deputy Chief was off duty.

In East Cleveland we often take on this role without any formal command-level training. The reason for this was the same reason that we were all used to hearing: "No money." It was a shame but, at times, it seemed like our fire department was managed like a slum lord manages his properties. The fire stations were always in a state of disrepair, the fire apparatus would sit idle for months at a time waiting for repair parts, and the condition of our firefighting bunker gear and equipment had fallen by the wayside. Although we were a poor city and one of the lowest paid department's in Ohio, our personal protective equipment had always been top notch. Sadly, even that had changed. New firefighters were often issued used, substandard gear. Some of the firefighting gear was donated to us from other neighboring departments. For these issues and the lack of formal training, again, the reason was the lack of money.

As newly promoted officers we were, for the most part, left to rely on the experience and knowledge that we had attained at our previous rank. We were basically thrown into the water and expected to either sink or swim. It's a hell of a lousy way to operate, but unfortunately that's how it was done at our department. I did receive some classroom training when I was promoted to lieutenant but, for acting captain and O.I.C., there was none.

As an O.I.C. I was now responsible for the well-being of the entire shift, or thirteen other men, as well as the operations at every fire and emergency scene. This really changes your mindset and your approach to the job, especially at the fire scene. One day you are a lieutenant, responsible for only the men who are riding on the engine or ladder truck that you are assigned to. Then the next day you are by yourself, driving the command car, and you have the responsibility of making sure everyone goes home safe to their loved ones in the morning. It just really made no sense to me that there was no formal training for a job requiring the ability to make critical, on-the-spot decisions that could potentially pose risk of injury, or even death, to your brother firefighters.

My preparation for the job of acting captain consisted of observing other captains and deputy chiefs who came before me. I thought of some of the guys who had served as the Fire Boss on my platoons over the course of my career. Some of the guys were yellers and screamers. They reminded me of a few football coaches I'd known who would get right up in your face if you made a mistake and chew your ass off. Other guys were calmer and not as forceful in their demeanor. And then you had guys who seemed like they didn't have the confidence in their ability to lead and, as a result, they would shy away from giving orders, preferring to let the platoon operate on its own. To me, this was a guy who could get firefighters hurt. I knew for sure that I didn't want to be like that.

I decided that I needed to make a commitment to the men and to myself to be a certain kind of O.I.C. Right or wrong, I made a conscious decision as to the type of O.I.C. I was going to be. I was not going to be a yeller and screamer because when this was done in the past, it usually made the firefighters more nervous than they already were and, as a result, more prone to making mistakes. I was also not going to be too laid back and quiet. This would only lead to the men questioning my confidence to command the fire scene. I was going to operate somewhere in between. I decided that I would be very clear and concise in every command that I gave and would not project any anxiety or overexcitement, no matter how much shit was hitting the fan. My goal was to have a calm, cool and, most importantly, a confident demeanor as an O.I.C. at the fire scene. I even decided that I would throw a little levity into some of the extreme fire scenes in order to calm the men a bit and help control the sky-high adrenaline levels. Experience really is the best teacher and, in East Cleveland, it was sometimes your only teacher. The bottom line for me was to use my past experiences to guide me and project confidence to the other firefighters.

I also thought it was very important for me to step aside and let the other line officers and firefighters do their jobs with minimal unnecessary interference from me. There were other O.I.C.'s in the past who would get on the radio and give an order every couple of minutes because I think it made them feel important. There is a fine line between directing the firefighting companies and splitting hairs with detailed, drawn-out radio communication. Radio communications between the O.I.C. and line officers needed to be brief and to the point. There were some things that didn't even need to be discussed over the radios at the fire scene and I didn't want to get caught up in unnecessary communication. There really is no room for over-inflated egos at the emergency scene!

My first two shifts as the O.I.C. were fairly uneventful, as far as the fires were concerned. Then, on my third opportunity as O.I.C., I was called on to command my first working fire scene. I was hoping that the first real fire would be something simple without too much confusion but, of course, that was not the case.

The call came in at 3:30 A.M. as someone attempting to set fire to the front porch of a house on Strathmore Avenue. But in the dispatcher's haste, I was not informed of a 3:29 A.M. call for an ambulance for a woman who had been struck by a car on Orinco Avenue, which ran parallel to and was one street west of Strathmore. This meant that we would be fighting the fire with twelve men, instead of the normal fourteen, because there were two men on the ambulance.

I was already in the command car heading to the scene when the police dispatcher called over the radio, "Police to fire." I responded, "Go ahead, police." Two more times the police dispatcher called over the radio in an attempt to contact me, and two times I radioed back but was not heard. This was a common occurrence. The police dispatcher did not have the volume turned up on the fire radio band and did not copy my transmission. I fumbled with a portable radio as I drove the command car, attempting to access the police band. Still, slightly groggy from waking suddenly from a deep sleep, I thought, "I don't want or need any more confusion right now!" I was close to the scene, so I gave up on trying to reach the police dispatcher.

Ladder Truck 121 arrived first. Lieutenant Dale Hoynacke sized up the situation and made the call. "Three-story wood frame house with smoke showing," he reported over the radio. "Working fire with visible flame on the A side, first floor. Truck 121 crew, bring a pre-connected hose line to the front door."

As I approached the fire scene, I parked the command car out of the way of the other incoming apparatus. I remembered to take command of the scene on the radio by saying, "Car 152 on the scene. 152 has Strathmore command." This was my baby now!

I got out of the command car, grabbed two portable radios, and moved toward the fire scene. I had to keep one radio on the fire ground band and the other on our normal frequency in case the police dispatcher attempted to reach me. As I approached, I could see a medium-sized fire burning on the front porch and encroaching into the front living room area. It looked like a fire that would be easily contained. It would have been, too, had it not been for the inability of the pump operator to get water pressure to the hose line. Lieutenant Hoynacke looked at me and said, "We're having a problem getting water."

"No shit, Dale!" I thought as I watched the fire steadily intensify while the veteran pump operator struggled to get pressure on the line. He then informed me that four kids lived in the house but everyone had gotten outside safely. That was a huge relief!

Just then I heard a dispatcher from Cleveland Heights, our neighboring community, attempting to contact me on the radio. "What the hell else could happen next?" I thought. Apparently, our police dispatcher called them to relay the initial radio message that they had been trying to give us as we left the engine house. Cleveland Heights informed me that the East Cleveland police dispatcher wanted to make sure that we had an ambulance responding to Orinoco for the female who was struck by the automobile. This was the first I was hearing of that emergency. I told the dispatcher to stand by. I was informed by our guys that we already had an ambulance responding to that location. I confirmed with Cleveland Heights that we were on scene at the vehicle accident. Damn, this was getting a little crazy!

The pump operator was still unable to get pressure on the line, so I told the crew to take the hose line off of Truck 121 and hook it up to a discharge on the next arriving engine. The pump operator shut down the line. By now the fire was really gaining headway, extending well into the living room and almost fully engulfing the front porch. Suddenly, as we were reconnecting the line to the engine discharge outlet, water came blasting out of the ladder truck's aerial discharge nozzle. The aerial discharge nozzle was attached to the 110-foot ladder and was designed to throw large volumes of water on buildings totally involved in fire for exterior operations. The nozzle was pointing straight down toward the street and about ten feet above it. Guys were scrambling to get out of the way of the master stream of water that was blasting down with enough force to knock any man down, splashing anyone in the vicinity. The ladder truck pump operator finally found out why there had been no pressure on the hose line. The aerial waterway valve had been left open, causing an air pocket to form in the piping and, as a result, reducing the water pressure.

By then I was about getting very pissed off from all the mistakes and confusion, but did my best to keep calm. We finally got the line connected to the engine with sufficient pressure on it. What had started out as a small fire on the exterior porch, was now a large porch fire and sizable interior house fire with excellent potential to spread to the upper floors. I called for two crews to take hose lines to the second and third floors and check for fire extension. Sure enough, the fire had extended slightly to the second floor but, fortunately, not to the third.

We now had adequate water pressure and were able to get the fire knocked in about fifteen minutes. The only thing left to do was make sure all of the hidden fire and hot embers were extinguished.

After the fire was under control, I began gathering information that was needed for the fire report. The story that I got from interviewing the tenant, some of the neighbors, and the police department, was bizarre to say the least. The house was occupied by four children between the ages of seven and thirteen, and their mother. The mother was not home when the fire broke out at 3:30 A.M. She showed up at approximately 4:00 am and was hysterical. Between the tears and sobs she explained to me that she had been at the laundromat when the fire broke out, which didn't make good sense. Why the hell would she leave her kids alone and be at the laundromat at 3:30 A.M.? The story got crazier at this point as I found out how the EMS call taken one minute prior to our fire call was somehow related.

Apparently, the woman who was struck by the automobile on Orinoco Avenue was friends with the mother of the four children on Strathmore. She was intoxicated and had an argument with her boyfriend in his car. When she got out of his car he decided to intentionally run her over. She ended up with some nasty head and facial abrasions, but would fully recover.

This same man who ran her over with his car then decided to go to the house on Strathmore, one block away, and set the house on fire. This was done out of spite because this woman was a friend of his girlfriend. He picked up a decorative landscaping brick from a yard across the street and threw it through the front window. He then proceeded to pour gasoline on the porch floor near the front windows and ignite it. The fire started there before extending though the front window and spreading into the living room. Luckily, the four children inside heard the brick crash through the window and managed to escape before the fire extended inside the house.

The guy who was responsible for all of this craziness was not the sharpest tool in the shed. He was arrested by the police department when he was seen standing on the sidewalk across the street, watching the fire that he started.

So much for a simple, easy first fire as officer in command. But that's the nature of the fire service. You never really know what to expect. You could work an entire twenty-four-hour shift without turning a wheel or, on the flip side, you could have fifteen to twenty EMS runs and three working fires in a single day. We are paid to be ready when emergencies occur.

After things calmed down and we got back to the engine house I felt good that, although some things had gone wrong and we faced some unforeseen challenges, the guys handled the adversity in a calm, professional, aggressive, effective manner. Mistakes were made and would be identified, critiqued, and corrected. The experience reaffirmed my belief that the O.I.C. is only as good as the men he commands. I understand that these guys are my most important weapon. They are also very brave and damn good at what they do. It made me feel very good to be able to lead a platoon of arguably the best firefighters in the State of Ohio. Because of the amount of working fires that we get in East Cleveland and the fact that every firefighter is expected to know every fire suppression job (no specialists), including operating the trucks, I would put our firefighters and officers up there against any other firefighters, anywhere in the country.

> *"Spanky ran in, Spanky ran out, then biff, bam, boom the house was on fire!"*
>
> *(citizen response when asked if she knew anything about her neighbor's house that was on fire)*

CHAPTER 18

War Story 5: *Sudden Death*

Spring was in the air on this bright, sunny April morning. It seemed like everyone was in a great mood, tired of the long winter doldrums. Then, at 9:30 A.M., a call came in on the 911 line. "We have a report of a male gunshot victim on Hower Avenue," said the East Cleveland police dispatcher. Our firefighter/dispatcher immediately called fire station Number Two and dispatched an ambulance to the scene. Because we staff our ambulances with only two paramedics and/or EMTs, we always send additional personnel on this type of emergency. In this case we sent Engine 112, a three-man crew, of which I was the lieutenant in charge that day.

Engine 112 was housed at fire station Number One and was closer to Hower Avenue than was the ambulance at station Two. The pace always picks up when there is a shooting and this day was no exception. Engine 112 and Squad 142 were on scene in less than three minutes. As we turned onto Hower from Euclid Avenue, we could see that the police had already blocked off the street. We pulled up to the police blockade and they removed the crime scene tape to let us through.

From the front seat of Engine 112 I saw a body lying face-down on the tree lawn. According to police, the victim had been shot in a car, then thrown from the vehicle to the location on the grass where he now laid. I got out of the front seat of Engine 112 and, along with my two men and the two EMS crew members, we immediately began assessing the condition of the victim and the treatment that would be required. After checking the victim's airway, securing his spine and applying a cervical collar to his neck, we log-rolled the victim onto a backboard. I looked into the lifeless eyes and realized that this was just a young kid, a teenager who, minutes earlier, was full of life. He was now desperately clinging to his life, with a bullet hole in his neck that was spilling blood out like a drinking fountain.

I looked into his eyes and there was nothing there. I was hoping to see him blink, but he didn't. I was looking for some sign of life, but saw none. We strapped the victim down securely then laid the backboard on top of the cot. We hurried him to the ambulance, then inside the rear where he could be treated and prepped for the trip to the hospital.

The EMS crew and my two crew members began to work on the victim. All of the guys worked together beautifully. Being from the "old school," I knew that my EMS skills were limited because I had never been required to work on the ambulance like all newly hired firefighters are now. I knew that in EMS emergencies like these, I needed to step aside and let my guys do their thing, even though I was technically in charge of this scene. Too many times I'd seen large egos get in the way when officers tried to bullshit their way around an EMS emergency scene and act like they knew exactly what to do. This is extremely counterproductive and I knew that the best way for me to assist in this emergency was to stay out of the way and only do basic things that don't require a high level of EMS skill.

The men worked together swiftly with no wasted motion. In a matter of minutes, they cut the clothes off his body, stopped the bleeding from the neck, attached the heart monitor, started two large-bore intravenous lines, and inserted a breathing tube with oxygen attached into the victim's throat. While this was going on, CPR was maintained. They worked hard trying to save this young kid.

The tension in the back of the ambulance was high. Then suddenly there was a blip on the heart monitor and the paramedic excitedly proclaimed that they had established a weak pulse from the victim. When he made that announcement, it gave everybody a sense of relief and hope for the young man. We wanted this young guy to make it so badly! Our guys had put their hearts and souls into saving his life. We now had a glimmer of hope and the next thing to do was to rush him to the hospital where a trauma team was anxiously awaiting our arrival.

The ambulance sped off and made its way to Huron Hospital, which was only about three minutes away from the emergency scene. The EMS crew arrived at the hospital and quickly whisked the victim into the hospital emergency room to the waiting trauma team of doctors, nurses, specialists, and student observers. In no time at all, we had him transferred from our cot to the emergency room table.

After the victim's care was transferred to the hospital staff, we nervously paced outside the operating room with not much dialogue between us. I noticed that the doctor in charge was directing a subordinate to cut into the victim's chest wall. I had never seen this done before so I went back into the operating room and attempted to find a decent vantage point where I could observe the procedure. The hospital staff rarely had a problem with the fire department paramedics and EMTs watching them work on patients, in fact they were very accommodating. For this particular patient there were probably fifteen to twenty people inside the operating room, either working or observing.

Under the instruction of the doctor in charge, the subordinate used a scalpel to cut open the young man's chest wall, then inserted spreaders to secure the opening that now exposed his quivering heart. The doctor in charge of the procedure was loud, very cocky, and impatient with the hospital staff. He seemed to be enjoying the fact that he was in charge. I could understand that there was no time for pussyfooting around in situations like this, but this guy went overboard. He had a very short fuse and seemed to intimidate some of the hospital staff with his continually shouting out orders. Although I had only been in the emergency room watching these procedures a few times, I knew that I didn't care for this guy's approach. I likened it to a fire scene and made this comparison: When the guy in charge is yelling and all geeked up, it makes others nervous and puts them in a mental state where they can't perform at their optimum level. I truly believe that when the person in charge is cool and calm under pressure, it rubs off on the rest of the crew and enables them to think clearly and work confidently.

Momentarily distracted by the head doctor's style, I was caught off guard and taken aback when, all of the sudden, he yelled, "Call it" – meaning he'd just pronounced the kid dead. I was shocked. I thought that the hospital staff should have spent more time and tried harder to save this kid. My guys had worked so hard on scene, doing their very best and performing expertly in a working environment that is much more adverse and challenging than a hospital emergency room. It just seemed to me that the doctor in charge had called this one too quickly and given up before trying everything possible.

Our glimmer of hope for this kid was now replaced with emptiness as we walked out of the operating room. I remember the doctor in charge looking me in the eyes, almost apologetically, and projecting something to me to justify ending the procedure and to acknowledge our concern for this victim. Because of his foreign accent I didn't quite understand what he said, but as I walked past him I felt like he was not nearly as concerned for this kid as we were. I honestly felt like the level of concern and hope for this kid had been much greater at the scene then it was in the emergency room. But I kept my mouth shut because they were the experts and I knew that I sure as hell was not.

Our mood afterwards was somber, at best. We become good at separating personal feelings for victims, but there is always some varying degree of effect on everyone. I only know for sure how much it affected me. After almost nineteen years on the job I'd become hardened to much of this. This incident bothered me because I expected a different outcome. I expected this kid to live. The thing that bothered me the most was how senseless it all was. I discovered later from police that this murder was drug related. These young, dope-selling, gang bangers don't realize how precious life is until they are rotting away in a jail cell, and that's a damn shame. Most of the parties involved in these crimes are usually gang rivals, friends, or acquaintances at one time or another.

It's hard to make any sense out of an incident like this. It's hard to find the positives that come out of this, if any. A young man was shot and thrown to the ground to die. The police, fire, and hospital staff used their skills to try and save a life, but were unable to do so. The feeling is hollow but you have to move on and continue to do your job. There will be days like this where you question how a human being can take another life so quickly, so easily, and many times, without remorse.

Psychiatric Patient to Firefighter: "I'm not going back to jail, playing football with a tampon, and an onion on my ass."

CHAPTER 19

Nine Dead in Charleston, South Carolina

On June 18, 2007, nine brave men paid the ultimate sacrifice when they lost their lives fighting a very tough fire in a sofa and furniture store in Charleston, South Carolina. What initially appeared to be a trash fire outside of the building, soon was discovered to be a raging monster inside the building, fueled by highly flammable toxic bedding materials. The building had no sprinkler system and the layout was a firefighter's nightmare, even before it became smoke-filled. The fire spread very quickly, as flames engulfed the warehouse and thick dark smoke and high heat conditions soon turned this scene into an extremely dangerous environment. In the end, nine courageous men became trapped in the building and died.

I did not intend for this chapter to be a part of this book but, out of respect for my fallen brothers, I am honoring them for their sacrifice to mankind and for the legacy that they left behind. This tragedy happened so suddenly and unexpectedly. To say it's not fair is the understatement of the century. One can only imagine the pain and suffering that all of the nine families, relatives, friends, and co-workers went through. To the families, from this author, from the East Cleveland Fire Department, from all fire departments around the United States, and from all fire departments all over the world, our hearts go out to you. We understand why these brave men did what they did on that fateful day. It is what we do as firefighters. To many it might not make sense now or maybe ever, but the reality of it is that it is our job to protect lives and property and it is the oath we take, and the promise we make, despite the risks involved. The bottom line and the underlying truth of the matter is, that if firefighters think people are inside a burning structure, we will do our best to rescue them, even if we have to put ourselves in harm's way. And to a lesser degree, we will enter a burning structure to save property too.

Experienced firefighters, who know how fires should be fought, will not publicly second-guess or criticize the bravery that our nine brothers displayed in the fire that took their lives so tragically. It is so easy to be a Monday-morning quarterback and say what should have been done instead of what actually was done. But, at the fire scene, you do not have the luxury of time to research and analyze each emergency situation. Things must happen fast and decisions must be made quickly. It is the nature of the job. It is the way we do things and research, study, and training over many, many years justifies these methods. It is the best way to do our job and I commend the Charleston Fire Department for doing the job according to their standard operating procedures and traditions. In East Cleveland, we would have done the same thing. As was the case on 9/11 in New York, they would never have sent firefighters into the twin towers if they had known the buildings would collapse. The same holds true for Charleston. They would never have had firefighters inside if they knew that it was too dangerous and firefighters would be killed. Sometimes things happen that are out of our control, and then tragedy strikes. Again, to the nine families of the fallen heroes, may God bless you and keep you safe and healthy. The world appreciates their sacrifice and realizes that they did not die in vain. We will never, ever forget them. May their memory stay with you, comfort you, and keep you strong.

During the memorial service held Friday June 22, 2007 at North Charleston Coliseum, more than 10,000 people gathered to honor the nine lost brave men, including representatives from more than 700 fire departments across the United States and Canada. Prior to the service, approximately 300 emergency service vehicles from throughout the state and nation, including 250 fire trucks and fire service vehicles, traveled in a 15-mile procession from downtown Charleston to the Coliseum to honor the fallen men. It's things like this that make me very proud to be a firefighter and appreciate the brotherhood that is shared worldwide.

Shortly after the tragedy, I had an excellent opportunity to pay my respects to the Charleston firefighters and represent the East Cleveland Fire Department. My brother Tom lives in Isle of Palms, South Carolina. This barrier island is only a fifteen-minute drive from Charleston. It just so happened that I was taking my family there on a vacation the first week of July. This was approximately two weeks after the fire on June 18, 2007 that killed the nine Charleston firefighters.

In East Cleveland, we too wanted to do something as a department to offer condolences and show our support. East Cleveland Firefighter Thomas Buth was the owner of a sign shop in Chardon, Ohio and he was more than happy to make a tee shirt for the Charleston Fire Department that honored the nine men. The shirt had our East Cleveland logo on the front and on the back, it read: "5-5-5-5" (This is the call sign for a firefighter's last alarm due to an on-duty death). Under that it read "In honor of our NINE fallen Charleston brothers. GONE BUT NEVER FORGOTTEN. East Cleveland Firefighters East Cleveland, Ohio." Along with this shirt, I also brought a couple of sympathy cards signed by our firefighters and cash for the families donated by our firefighters. I felt good about being able to do this small thing for them, but at the same time I was very apprehensive about going because it had only been two weeks since the tragedy.

My family arrived in Isle of Palms, South Carolina on Saturday June 30, 2007. The local support for the nine firefighters was incredible, and not just in Charleston. In Isle of Palms I saw a fireman's boot in a couple of retail stores for donations to the families. A restaurant was selling memorial tee shirts with the proceeds going to the families. I was informed that the cash donated at that time was already over a million dollars and expected to go considerably higher. It is so refreshing to see people step up to help out in tragic events such as this. It was also nice to know that the families would be taken care of financially but, at the same time, it was bittersweet because of their loss.

On the day that I was making the trip to the main fire station at 46½ Wentworth Street in downtown Charleston, I called the engine house for directions. I spoke with one of the assistant Chief's on the telephone. He was very friendly and helpful with the directions. Even though I'd never met him before, he was very receptive to me visiting the station and told me to park in the fire department lot and come right up the back steps into his office.

As I proceeded on my short trip to Charleston, my mind wandered. I tried to put myself in the place of the people who I was going to visit. I felt uneasy because two weeks was really not much time to get over such a loss. I understand that firefighters, EMS workers, and police are usually conditioned to seeing some pretty bad things on a fairly regular basis and, because of this, they become hardened to some of the emotions that are normally felt during these situations. But this was very different. These were their own people. These guys were like family. They ate, slept, and worked together. Many socialized together. They socialized with each other's families, black and white, young and old, men and women, you name it. It's one thing being able to separate tragic events with personal feelings when it's someone who you don't know. But when it's a friend or someone you are close to and care for, well that's another story.

I drove over the Cooper River Bridge and exited on Bay Street. I made my way downtown and turned right on Wentworth Street. I proceeded until I arrived at

46½ Wentworth. This was the address of the Charleston Fire Department's main station. It was a very old building with all the markings of the typical old-school traditional firehouse. As I passed through a rear door, I noticed some antique fire apparatus parked inside the bay area. The engine house was very clean and in a good state of repair, despite the age of the building. It looked like at one time they had the poles, of old, that the early stations used for firefighters to slide down from the second floor into the apparatus room on the first floor. The holes were now covered up and the poles were taken out. We still have and use them at East Cleveland Fire Department station #1 to this day. Most of the fire trucks were not in house at this time and I didn't see anybody on the first floor. After a short look around, I walked up the stairs to the second floor and into the administrative offices.

The door to the Assistant Chief's office was open so I walked up to the door and looked inside. Assistant Chief Ed

Bath saw me standing there and waved me in. He was very accommodating and friendly. It was obvious that he was busy and in the middle of a project on his computer, but he took time out to talk with me.

I introduced myself then sat across from his desk and expressed my condolences for their loss. It's always hard to find the right words to say to someone who has just suffered the loss of a loved one. This was more difficult because they lost not one, but nine lives in that fire. I gave him the tee shirt and cards from our department and he was very appreciative. I told Assistant Chief Bath that I wanted him to know that the East Cleveland Fire Department was behind them and that we would have attacked the fire just as they did. He was a very extroverted guy and easy to talk to.

Assistant Chief Bath seemed eager to talk to me about the fire which surprised me somewhat. I think he was at ease because we shared a common bond and he knew that I wasn't in there to second guess anyone, unlike some of the local newspapers and media. He told me some things about the fire that were contrary to what was being reported in the media. He told me that the firefighters were actually killed by a huge flashover. Prior to this, all of the reports that I had heard of or read about said that the men were killed in a collapse. He also stated that at least one of the firefighters was trapped and running out of air. He knew that he was about to die and he transmitted these words that I'll never forget over a portable radio, "tell my wife that I love her." Those were his last words and, although I wasn't even there, I will never forget that. My worst nightmare is getting trapped or disoriented and running out of air inside of a heavily involved burning structure. I really do not want to go down like that and I felt absolutely horrible for those firefighters and, particularly, for the one who had time to think about it before he died. Assistant Chief Bath said that they really weren't supposed to talk too much about the fire and I would never have put this information in the book if it hadn't already become public information through the investigative report.

I could see the anguish and pain on Assistant Chief Bath's face, and I could hear it in his voice. He spoke of going to four funerals in one day and said it was the worst thing that he had ever experienced. He said that eight of the nine men who died were from his engine house and that he'd worked with at least one of them for over thirty years. He also said the Fire Chief was getting a lot of flak and criticism from media and various outside agencies and that it would get much worse before it got better. We talked for about 15 minutes and when I got up he shook my hand and gave me a hug. I felt good for showing support but, at the same time, somewhat empty because I think that I inadvertently caused this man to go back to the tragedy in his mind at a point in time when he was trying to move on and grasp onto some sense of normalcy. As I left his office I wondered if this grief-stricken man would continue much longer on the job. He had the necessary years toward retirement, should he opt to do so. It wouldn't surprise me if this incident would force his hand in hope of ending the nightmare that he would have to relive in his mind for the rest of his life.

I'd hoped to be able to speak to some of the firefighters, but they were out on a training detail. After speaking with the Assistant Chief, I was almost relieved that the firefighters were out of the engine house. I realized that it was too soon after the tragedy and that they needed time to grieve among themselves and their families without being bothered by people they didn't know. At least that was my take on the situation.

I'd also wanted to talk to the Fire Chief. I read in the Charleston newspaper about the fire and also about Chief

Rusty Thomas. He seemed like a real dedicated professional who knew his job very well and genuinely cared for the men and women who worked for him. When I arrived at the fire station I was told that he was out of quarters but when I came down the engine house stairs on my way out, I saw him at the apparatus bay door entrance. He was speaking with some citizens on the sidewalk. In the short time I was there, I'd noticed people passing by, looking, talking among themselves, and taking pictures. Most of the passersby knew of the tragedy and were paying respect and showing support, each in their own way. I wanted a chance to speak briefly with Chief Thomas and as the citizens on the sidewalk turned to leave, I approached him.

I introduced myself and offered my condolences on behalf of the East Cleveland Fire Department. I told him the same thing that I told Assistant Chief Bath. I told him that we would have attacked the fire in the same manner that they did. It was important to me to convey to him that I had his back. He was being unfairly second-guessed in the media and by city officials. As is the case in tragedies where lives are lost, society has deemed that there must be a whipping boy, a scapegoat, someone to point fingers at and place blame on. Well I just wanted Chief Thomas to know that, although I wasn't present at the fire, I was on his side and I understood why they did what they did.

He really appreciated the support, especially coming from a man in the same business. He explained to me that when their initial apparatus pulled up on the fire scene, he had two officers, each with over thirty years' experience, in charge of crews and making calls. I knew that to have this much experience on the initial attack is a luxury that is rare. It is also comforting and reassuring to any Fire Chief at the fire scene. He told me that they felt the right decisions were made, but the conditions changed so rapidly. It is so easy to second guess, but many times unexpected changes suddenly occur during firefighting operations. This type of fire is not common so many more things can go wrong because of the size and makeup of the structure.

Chief Thomas knew that he was going to be put under a microscope with intense internal investigation, media, and outside agency scrutiny. There will be mandatory standard operating procedure changes. As a result, the Charleston Fire Department will benefit from these changes. They will get better. That will be one positive that will come out of this and will be a part of the legacy of the Charleston 9.

Our short conversation ended when another passerby brashly interrupted us to discuss with the Chief why he hadn't returned his call about selling memorial plaques that he'd designed. The Chief was extremely polite and accommodating to this citizen who I thought was out of line at a time when it was totally inappropriate. I watched how Chief Thomas handled this guy and as I looked in his eyes I could see that, even though he was carrying on a conversation with this citizen, he was a million miles away thinking of the tragedy. I decided to excuse myself and leave, knowing that he was overwhelmed and everybody wanted a piece of him. I said goodbye to the Chief, who was still talking with the citizen. In his mannerisms and his facial expressions, I could tell that he was very stressed out, just as Assistant Chief Bath was. I felt really sorry for him because, not only did he lose nine firefighters, but he also will be the guy who will get the brunt of the criticism and blame. This nightmare will also stay with him for the rest of his life. As I turned to leave, Chief Thomas stopped me and said, "Wait, where did you say you were from?" I replied "East Cleveland". He nodded his head as if to say "thanks for the support East Cleveland, I won't forget you." He probably won't forget this small gesture of support but I know for sure that I'll never forget Chief Thomas for what he went through and will have to go through being the point man of the Charleston Fire Department. May God bless him, the Charleston Firefighters and their families and give them the strength to get through the worst tragedy they have ever faced in the history of the Charleston fire service.

"All gave some; some gave all."
(slogan honoring the Charleston 9)

CHAPTER 20

Bizarre Events & Outrageous Behavior

Deputy Chief Tom "The Bomb" Flowers once said, "The City of East Cleveland is a place where parallel lines intersect." He meant that it seemed a different set of rules applied for this city and, at times, there seemed to be no rules at all.

Coming from Akron, a city of almost 200,000 people, I thought I'd seen a lot of crazy things. But the truth of the matter is that, compared to East Cleveland, I hadn't seen anything! My cousin, John Hart, who'd previously worked for the East Cleveland Fire Department, told me shortly before I was hired that I would experience just about everything possible in this city during the course of my career as a firefighter. Boy, was he right! Eventually I got to the point where I just said, "Nothing that happens here surprises me anymore!"

TAKE 1:

Without going into detail and naming names, these are a few of the things that have happened in East Cleveland over the last twenty-plus years and have made what I call the Working Fire Hall of Fame:

1. A former mayor allegedly stabbed her husband to death.
2. Another former mayor went to jail for money laundering and accepting bribes.
3. Yet another former mayor made national news when photos of him dressed like a woman made their way to the TV channels just prior to the election. (He lost.)
4. A former city council president was shot in the hand while allegedly soliciting a gay prostitute.
5. A city council president was arrested for soliciting sex from a minor gay male.
6. A city housing inspector was fired and arrested the same day that our fire department extinguished a fire at his house and, after the smoke cleared, found a nice crop of marijuana under grow lights in his attic.
7. A former firefighter called in sick an entire day late and used the excuse that he was unable to call off on time because he'd been kidnapped and locked in the trunk of his car. He was eventually fired.
8. A former firefighter used to pull outside fire alarm boxes, then go to the fire station when the firefighters left the building and steal the $5 or so in the change box that was kept for the soda pop machine. He was later forced to resign for other infractions.
9. A former firefighter sucker-punched another firefighter when he was reading a newspaper, fracturing bones in his face in six places, resulting in two reconstructive surgeries. The assailant was charged with felonious assault but pled guilty to a lesser reckless assault charge. Believe it or not, he was not suspended from the fire department, even for one

day. He was, however, forced to resign and given six months' probation from the common pleas court.

10. A former firefighter went to jail after shooting someone in the leg who was trying to steal his car. This was a shame because he was a good man but the judge was not interested in giving any breaks to firefighters, even though many firefighters, both black and white, testified on his behalf.

11. Fire Station #2 has about fifteen bullet holes in the apparatus room doors from the gang bangers in the neighborhood.

12. Bulletproof glass was installed in the officer's room at Fire Station #2 after a bullet whizzed through the window on a Saturday afternoon, nearly striking Lieutenant Mike Gunn. It missed him by about eighteen inches.

13. The parking lot at Fire Station #2 had to be gated and padlocked because our cars were getting stolen from the lot.

14. Fire Station #2 was broken into on different occasions and items were stolen. There was even one instance when a guy broke in and stole some things when the firefighters were asleep in the building. He was not caught. We joked about it because one of the firefighters there at the time was a martial artist who claimed to be able to walk on rice paper without making a sound. Yet he couldn't hear some burglar breaking into the engine house through a window. We told him that he was probably so scared that he was hiding underneath his blankets with his teeth chattering.

15. In the same year, two firefighters' sons were shot multiple times. One of them was shot seven times. Thankfully they both recovered from their wounds.

16. A lieutenant who was giving a training class fell asleep during his own lecture.

17. An officer came up with his own solution for a radio that wasn't working properly. He had just come out of a raging arson fire in a vacant apartment building. He was a bit irate because his crew was unable to advance the attack line due to storage items inside the building that were blocking their way. His O.I.C. informed him that he had been trying to reach him on the radio but had gotten no response. Out of frustration, he threw the radio onto the concrete sidewalk as hard as he could, smashing it into pieces. He looked up at his O.I.C. and deadpanned, "This fucking piece of shit radio doesn't work."

And finally…

18. A male EMS patient, who was extremely high on PCP, was found upon arrival of our ambulance crew, attempting to have sex with the exhaust pipe of an automobile!

In no certain order, here are some other short stories from my career in East Cleveland. A lot of the stories are unusual. Some are funny. Some are amazing. Some are downright brutal and typify man's inhumanity to man. But all are true and were things that I'd never experienced previously and most likely, never will again.

TAKE 2:

EMS Squad 141 crew members Bryan Knights and Alafia Hairston responded to a stabbing call. East Cleveland police were already on scene and had broken up a fight between a man and a woman. Upon arrival, EMS first noticed the woman in handcuffs outside of the apartment in the hallway. They were informed by police that she stabbed her boyfriend in the head with a steak knife.

They walked into the suite and saw the victim with his back toward them, casually sweeping the kitchen floor. Hairston and Knights looked at the guy then at each other in disbelief. Knights whispered quietly to Hairston, "Is that a knife stuck in that dude's head?" The guy turned toward them and angrily asked what the hell they were doing in his apartment. He was visibly upset and wanted an answer to his question. Knights looked at him and said, "Man, do you know that you have a knife stuck in your head?" The man was oblivious and asked Knights what the hell he was talking about.

Knights grabbed a mirror and held it up so the guy could see the knife, buried to the handle in the side of his head. The guy almost fainted. After that his demeanor changed completely and he was more than happy to let Hairston and Knights treat him and transport him to Huron Hospital.

Apparently, the couple had gotten into a drunken brawl and it got ugly. During the fight the woman grabbed a cheap kitchen steak knife and planted it into the top of the guy's head, but it pierced the scalp and slid down the side of his head, never entering the skull. That, and a fair amount of liquor, was why the guy didn't know he had a knife in his head. Incidentally, he went on to make a full recovery.

TAKE 3:

It was about 7:30 A.M. one hot, humid summer morning. My shift at the fire department started at 8:30 A.M., but I liked to get to work early, get a cup of coffee, and read the sports page from the Cleveland Plain Dealer. As I drove across the border from Cleveland into East Cleveland, I noticed something strange going on about a block ahead of me. It was normally pretty quiet at this time of the day but as I got closer, I noticed that something pretty bizarre was happening just in front of me, in broad daylight.

I pulled up to a stop sign and waited there, looking ahead, somewhat dumbfounded by what I saw. Directly in front of me was a car headed in the opposite direction driving at a speed of about twenty to thirty miles per hour, with a man spread across the hood, holding onto the top edge of the hood with his left hand and furiously punching the windshield with his right. As the car approached mine, I could hear the man shouting, "You fucking bitch, you fucking bitch, you fucking bitch!" As she passed, I could see the woman's face. She appeared perfectly calm.

I didn't stick around to see how things ended up and could only shake my head as I continued on to work.

TAKE 4:

Summer of 1994, a Sunday morning at about 3 A.M. The East Cleveland police dispatcher reported that a car hit a tree head-on at a high rate of speed and caught fire on Lee Road. Dispatch also reported that the car was driven by a group of teenagers who abandoned the car and were seen fleeing the scene immediately after the crash.

Engine 114 responded. Upon reaching the top of the hill, we could see the smoke and fire from the vehicle, which was now almost fully involved with flames. We pulled up just past the car so that we were upwind from the smoke. It appeared to be just another car fire.

We stretched out a hose line and proceeded to extinguish the flames. Then, what had seemed to be a routine car fire suddenly took an unexpected twist. When the smoke cleared and we opened the passenger door we were blown away by what we saw inside. Pinned underneath the passenger side dashboard was a dead body, sitting upright and burnt beyond recognition. The legs had been pinned under the dash from the impact of the crash, trapping the victim in the burning wreckage. We learned later that the victim was a 17-year-old girl.

This was the first time I'd seen a burnt-up body. It was not a pretty sight. In fact, it was quite a grisly scene, especially since it was the first one for me. This poor girl had been left in the burning car by her so-called friends to die a horrifying death. Nobody deserves such a terrible fate, especially a young kid who had her whole life ahead of her.

This was one scene I'd always remember. There were four others in the car who ran away and left her there to burn to death. To this day, I still don't know if the other teenagers were caught and charged with any crimes. Their punishment will be the guilt they will carry for the rest of their lives.

TAKE 5:

At 8:20 A.M., ten minutes prior to a shift change, we received a call from the police dispatcher requesting an ambulance to respond to a call regarding an eighty-five-year-old diabetic man who was being combative with his wife. His wife was also in her eighties. Two police officers were already on scene. Apparently, the man's wife was the one who had placed the call for assistance. The police asked our paramedics to check the man out to make sure that his vital signs were okay.

Firefighter-Paramedics Jeff Pizzuli and Don Ross responded to the scene and were greeted by two police officers who briefed them as to what had transpired so far. They stated that the man had been drinking beer for a while and was already pretty buzzed, even though it wasn't even 8:30 in the morning yet. They said that his wife was worried because he was being very belligerent toward her.

When they attempted to take his vital signs and assess his medical condition, he became combative. He would not calm down or cooperate, so one of the police officers pinned him and held him down to enable the medics to work. The old guy continued to struggle and fight as they took blood pressure and blood sugar levels. The medics determined that the patient was medically sound and the belligerence was the direct result of being very drunk.

The police officer finally got off the man as the paramedics finished their work. The man was still yelling and screaming until Pizzuli looked him directly in his eyes and said, "You've got two choices. You're either going to the hospital or to jail, so what's it going to be?" The old man finally shut up and settled down for a few seconds. He looked at Pizzuli as if he had finally caught on. They all thought that he was now going to behave himself.

What happened next caught the police officers and the paramedics completely off guard. The old guy glared at Pizzuli and then at Ross. Both paramedics were white guys. The police officers and the elderly couple were black. The old guy then made this statement that blew them all away; "You motherfucking crackers! You crackers are here to take my house. Go ahead, cracker, take my fucking house!"

Pizzuli just looked at the man in disbelief and said, "Well sir, that's really not what we had in mind. We're actually here to help you."

The old guy didn't want to hear it and he continued to rant and rave. The medics did their job and determined that the guy should get a ride to the hospital in a police cruiser instead of the ambulance. The police officers took the man to the hospital in handcuffs to be evaluated and sleep it off. They all had a good laugh when they got outside.

Take 6:

It was a warm July afternoon in 2005. The hot line at station #2 rang and we were told to respond to a house fire on Shaw Avenue. I immediately knew that our ladder company would be arriving first on scene because our station was just a couple of blocks away. As I dressed into my turnout gear, I started to prepare myself mentally for leading my crew in to attack this potential house fire.

At this point in my career I knew that the information that is telephoned in to us isn't always accurate. I also understood that you can't rely on the emotions of the caller to determine the legitimacy of the emergency. For instance, you could have a caller completely freaking out about smoke and fire in the building and when you get there you find out that it was just a pan of food that was burnt up. On other occasions, you may get a caller who is completely calm and informs you, very nonchalantly, that their house is on fire. Your instincts tell you that this is a false alarm but, sure enough, when you arrive the house is on fire.

In less than two minutes we were out of the engine house. We pulled up to the address on Shaw Avenue, As the officer in charge of Ladder Truck 121, it was my job to get out of the truck first, investigate, and then give a radio report back to my crew and the other incoming fire apparatus.

Before I exited the truck, I sized up the scene: "Three-story, wood-frame house with nothing showing on three sides." I then walked to the back of the house and could not believe what I saw. I noticed a smoldering object in the back yard, about ten feet from the back of the house. As I got closer I realized that this was a fairly large, dead dog that had been set on fire. It appeared to be a Rottweiler, and it was badly burned up. There was also a large kitchen knife next to the dog's body. The skin was split in different areas from the extreme heat, and the smell of burnt flesh filled the air. This was a pretty grisly sight, especially if you were an animal lover.

I then gave a radio report that I'd never given nor even heard before, and probably never will again: "EC-2 to all incoming fire apparatus, we have a dog fire, out on arrival.

Truck 121 crew can handle. All other companies can go in service."

There was a long pause, then the command officer radioed back, "Um, you were broken up, can you repeat your traffic?" I laughed to myself, then repeated my previous transmission. Another pause, then someone barked into the radio. I knew that these guys were still going to stop by to look at this even though I called them off. It's not often that you get a call for a "dog fire."

It was hard to imagine how anyone could do this to an animal. We discovered later that some kids were seen fleeing the scene just prior to our arrival. What we could not determine was whether the dog was burnt alive or had died and the kids set its corpse on fire. I really didn't know what they were going to do with the knife. It was a bit disturbing and made me wonder what was going on in their minds.

The topper to the whole story is how the dog's body was disposed of. Since we didn't have an animal control department in the city, the command officer chose to improvise. He ordered the two junior firefighters to wrap the dog up in a blanket and set it on the back of the fire engine. They were then told to take the animal to fire station #1 parking lot and throw it in the dumpster. I really didn't agree with this decision but, what the hell, this was East Cleveland and nothing surprised me anymore.

It reminded me of a time early on in my career when I pulled a half-dead cat out of a smoke-filled building and gave it to a paramedic. When I returned later I asked the paramedic if the cat survived. I'll always remember his exact words. He said: "No, the cops shot it and threw it in the dumpster." I was dumfounded but soon came to learn that things don't always go by the book when you work in the city of East Cleveland.

Firefighter: "What is your medical history?"

Patient: "I had Spider Monkey Jesus."

Firefighter: "Do you mean Spinal Meningitis?"

Patient: "Yeah, that's it!"

CHAPTER 21

The Edge

Not all people are born with the mental and physical traits that are necessary to become an accomplished firefighter. By an accomplished firefighter, I mean an individual who has the nerve to go deep inside a burning structure and stay composed and focused, even when things go haywire. I like to refer to this characteristic as "the edge." It is similar to an athlete having the "X" factor in his or her given sport. It is really hard to accurately define exactly what it means to have the edge, but I honestly believe that it is a quality that you are either born with or you are not. It is more of an instinctive human trait as opposed to a learned behavior.

It is against human nature to charge into a burning building when everybody else is running out. The large percentage of fires that firefighters encounter are, for the most part, "room and content" fires. Room and content fires are confined to the structural members and contents of the room where the fire originated. Fires of this nature are extinguished quickly and usually provide firefighters with a good adrenaline rush, but do not normally test the boundaries of their nerves and courage. The fires that test your mettle are the ones that burn through the ceilings and walls of the room where they originated and extend upward and/or outward to the floor above and sometimes beyond.

At a fire of this nature there is a much higher risk factor and it is considerably more dangerous. Fire travel is not always predictable, especially when the interior walls and ceilings structural members have been altered. Chasing a fire like this involves very hard work, opening up holes in these void spaces during extremely high heat conditions and near zero visibility. Fatigue is unavoidable, both mentally and physically. It is at this point of fatigue that a firefighter is the most vulnerable in losing the edge. I have heard numerous accounts from firefighters over the years who've had a brush with death and, although they didn't say so, I knew that their edge was compromised, to some degree. It is human nature and unavoidable that your thinking is altered when you experience an incident in which you were injured or almost died.

In the first twenty years of my career it happened to me twice. The first time was at a house fire where I almost ran out of air before just barely making it outside. Had I chosen to proceed in another direction, I could have easily died in that house fire. That moment in time was, without a doubt, the worst feeling that I've ever experienced. In that short instance I realized that if I chose the wrong path, there would be a good chance I would run out of air and die from asphyxiation. I had never felt so helplessly all alone in my entire life. I just plain got lucky that day! I knew that my edge had been compromised by this brush with death. I would never fight fires with the same cocky confidence that I had prior to that incident. I had been too confident, to the point where I made a couple of avoidable mistakes that almost cost me my life. To be honest, my edge needed to be compromised in order for me to become safer and smarter in my approach to the job.

My second experience with having my edge compromised came after eighteen years on the job, after I'd been promoted to lieutenant. In East Cleveland, lieutenants are in charge of all crew members on their assigned apparatus. At the time of this incident there were four crew members, including me. It is the officer's job to make sure that he and his men are safe and they go home to their loved ones after their shift is over. On this day we almost lost a couple of guys, myself included.

It happened at a large apartment building fire on Wymore Avenue. After our initial fire attack our low air alarms were sounding, signaling us to leave the building and get a fresh air tank. I was unable to find my way out and I was with a new man who was also running out of air. We made the critical mistake of leaving the hose line which, if we followed it in reverse, was our way to find the door to the outside. We talked to each other but neither of us knew the way to the outside through the thick smoke. We made a second critical mistake by not staying together. This was my fault. It was my job, as a lieutenant, to make sure we stayed together, but I got caught up focusing on finding the way out. When I finally found the door I turned around to find that the new man was not with me. There were a few firefighters standing by the door and I asked them if the new man came out. They said no, and when I heard that, I was overcome with anxiety. I told the firefighters that the new man was still inside and to get in there and find him immediately. I was unable to assist as my air tank was now fully exhausted. I knew that time was of the essence!

I waited nervously by the door as the firefighters searched for the new man. In what seemed like a lifetime, two minutes passed by and a veteran firefighter came through the door with the new man, safe and sound! I was never so relieved in all my life! This easily could have been a very different, tragic ending, and it would have resulted in a never-ending nightmare for me.

As a result of this incident, my edge was once again affected, but not to the point where I feared going into a fire. The fact that one of my crew members could have been injured or killed put an exclamation point on the incident. It made me much more cerebral when entering a burning structure. After that, I tried to consider all possible worst-case scenarios for each incident. I took a few extra seconds with the exterior scene size-up, looking at doors and windows as possible escape routes before entering the burning structure. I tried to balance the risks and rewards of each incident, then act in the best interests of my crew first, then the citizens, and finally the property that we were trying to save.

I honestly believe that having my edge compromised made me a better officer and tactician. My confidence was affected, but it was for the better because it made me more cautious. I do, however, miss the cocky feeling of being invincible when entering a dangerous working fire environment. Early on in my career I didn't think of dying in a fire. I only thought of penetrating deep, finding the flames, and slaying the beast. The change in my mental status can be attributed to the past brushes with death and also to growing older. I'm not ashamed to admit that as you get closer to retirement age, it is only normal to proceed more cautiously and carefully as you think of getting through the end of your career safely.

The important thing to realize is that when the edge is compromised to the point where you fear going into a fire, then it is time to call it quits. It is at this point that you become a liability to your fellow firefighters. In a busy fire department such as East Cleveland's, a line officer cannot fly under the radar forever if his edge is lost. It will become apparent to others if this happens. In the final analysis it is up to each firefighter or officer to call it quits when he loses the edge. It is their responsibility to do so but it is also the most difficult thing that they will ever have to do.

Losing the edge can be both good and bad. It depends on how traumatic your experience was. In my case I was very lucky, and I learned great lessons without getting injured in the process. There have been many other brave, aggressive, experienced East Cleveland firefighters, in similar situations, who got disoriented in fires and ran completely out of air and were traumatized, badly burned, or injured. Of those firefighters, (a few of them my co-workers), some were able to rescue themselves or were rescued by other firefighters. Their experiences were much, much more traumatic than mine. They were about as close to death as possible and, as a result, their edge was severely compromised or lost altogether.

If you haven't had a similar experience, it's harder to understand losing any part of the edge. On the other hand, if you've been through a close call on the job where you almost died, and you say it didn't affect you mentally in any way, you are lying. If you are a human being and you have a pulse, any brush with death will have some lasting effect on you. The severity of the situation, and the physical and mental effects, will determine not only if your edge is compromised, but also to what degree.

Retired East Cleveland Firefighter Bob Bastian's normal response to a verbal assault: "Chew it, Pork Pig"!

CHAPTER 22

War Story 6: *Triple-header*

A tripleheader in the fire service is fighting three working fires in a single 24-hour shift. To my knowledge a tripleheader is as rare to firefighters as a triple play is to baseball players. But most firefighters who spent their entire careers in East Cleveland can lay claim to at least one. I had a couple tripleheaders and even had one 24-hour shift with four pretty good working house fires..

But I would like to share not the one that I experienced, but instead the tripleheader that A shift had between December 1st and 2nd, 2007. The firefighters on A shift definitely earned their money that day. As a matter of fact, the firefighters on B shift ended up spending the first nine hours of their shift on December 2nd extinguishing and overhauling A shift's third fire of the tripleheader.

The first fire occurred at 7:04 P.M. on Hazel Street. This was your basic room-and-contents house fire. The guys got inside quickly and extinguished the flames in about fifteen minutes. Including the salvage and overhaul operations, they were on scene for one hour. An accurate benchmark for a real good working fire is about two hours on scene time, so this first fire was a good warm up for the firefighters.

The second fire occurred at 10:17 P.M. on East 135th Street. This was also a house fire but, in this case, the flames extended from the room where it started to the floor above and slightly beyond. This fire required substantially more work than the first one in order to extinguish the flames. But the firefighters worked very hard and after all was said and done, they had spent two hours at this fire scene before returning to quarters. By the time they got all of the air bottles filled, the reports finished, and the tools and equipment back in service, it was almost 2:30 A.M. At this point everybody was wet, dirty, sweaty, sore, cold, and very tired. If they had been able to stay in quarters the rest of the night, they would have gotten about five hours of sleep.

Well, after roughly two and a half hours of sleep, the station house alarm bells sounded again, this time at 5:07 A.M. It is a terrible feeling when the bells go off when you are that tired and in such a deep sleep. The very last thing you want to do is to put your cold, wet, dirty, smelly, turnout gear back on and go out again into the cold, dark December morning air for another fire. But that is exactly what these guys had to do, and it would be about six more long hours until they were finally allowed to go home.

You've heard of saving the best for last? Well, without a doubt the third fire of the shift was the best, or worst, depending on who you talk to about it. The third fire was started by the improper use of a space heater and was called in to East Cleveland Fire dispatch just after 5 A.M. The caller stated that there was light smoke in the hallway of their apartment building. The station house alarm bells were activated, then all companies responded to Superior Avenue, the Rockefeller Building, which had twenty-two apartment suites on four floors.

The Rockefeller was built in the early 1900s. It had the old-style light beige brick facade exterior walls and a flat tar-and-gravel built-up roof. The interior construction consisted of wooden floors and ceilings with plaster and lath walls covering the interior wooden studs. It was a solidly built and well-maintained structure.

The building was grandfathered in under older fire codes that did not require it to have a fire sprinkler system in the building. It did, however, have hard-wired smoke detectors, manual pull stations and audible fire alarms throughout the building, tied into a working alarm system. The front of the building faced due east and the interior hallway layout of the structure was shaped like an "I". The front hallway ran north to south, connecting at midpoint to the center hallway that ran east to west, then finally connecting at midpoint to the rear hallway that, like the front, ran north to south. The building had one interior and one exterior staircase. The interior staircase was located approximately thirty feet from the front entrance, near the area where the front hallway intersected with the middle hallway. The exterior staircase was in the rear of the building, near the northwest corner. This staircase served as a fire escape for the building occupants.

One factor that added a bit of confusion to this incident was the way the floors were named and numbered. The first floor was referred to as the ground floor. In order to get to the first floor, you had to go up a flight of stairs to the next level. In most buildings this would be the second floor. This can be confusing as it pertains to being accountable for firefighter crew locations when not all personnel are on the same page with the terminology.

Just minutes after receiving the report of smoke in the hallway, all East Cleveland fire apparatus arrived at the Rockefeller building. Reserve Engine 114 was first on the scene. Lieutenant Jerry Jones was in charge of Engine 114 on this day and he was told by the custodian that the fire was on the second floor in the rear (southwest) corner of the structure. After investigation, Jones found that thick, black smoke had banked down to the floor at the top of the stairwell on the second floor. So much for "light smoke in the hallway!" Engine 114 crew deployed a hose line to attack the fire.

Firefighter Dave Worley, who was the nozzleman for this fire, grabbed the hose line from Engine 114 and, along with Lieutenant Jones, proceeded through the front door and up the staircase to the second floor. The second floor was actually the third story in this case and they'd already played out quite a bit of hose line even before they got into the hallway on the second floor. This was an unusually long lay of attack hose and required assistance from at least two other firefighters for them to reach the seat of this fire.

At the top of the stairwell, they donned their air masks and proceeded into and down the hallway in an attempt to find the fire. Initially they walked, but were soon forced to crawl through zero visibility and rapidly increasing heat conditions. At first the heat was bearable but, as time passed, it quickly became hotter and hotter. These men were being put to the ultimate test that a firefighter will face. And keep in mind that this entire crew of fourteen men had already been through a very long day, including two fires and numerous EMS runs in the previous twenty-plus hours. Mental and physical fatigue was unavoidably going to be a factor at this emergency scene.

They continued into the hallway toward the rear of the building, advancing the hose line as they edged forward. They made it all the way to the rear hallway, then took the left turn around the corner. The fire was in the apartment about forty feet straight ahead of them. They could see the glow of the flames and also hear the crackling sounds of the fire that was now free burning, having vented out an exterior window.

They attempted to move forward but were unable to do so as the slack in the hose line suddenly tightened up. Lieutenant Jones called for more hose but apparently the entire 400-foot length of hose was either completely played out or hung up somewhere in the dark, smoke-filled hallways. It was not exactly clear if the men shagging the hose for them initially knew it was all played out or if they had attempted to see if there was any slack hose available. Because this hose line was unable to be advanced at this critical point in the fire attack, the fire became so hot that one could suffer from thermal burns even though the fire was about thirty to forty feet away. It was now to the point where it was time for the interior crews to back out quickly or risk serious injury.

This fire had suddenly changed from an offensive to a defensive attack, with firefighter safety being the number-one priority. An experienced firefighter can tell when the heat in the environment is so extreme that it is time to get out. They know this because the heat is so intense that it will force you low to the ground as you feel your face and ears burning. Knowing when to back out is critical because if you let your pride get in the way, the consequences can be deadly. There is absolutely no shame in backing out when a fire gets too hot. In this case, these guys had no choice.

To make matters worse, in the confusion over coming up short with the hose line, Lieutenant Jones and Firefighter Worley became separated from the hose line. This was an extremely serious situation now because the hose line was their way out of the building. They were very deep into this structure and conditions were now life threatening. Having a hose line to guide you outside is reassuring, but it is not a guarantee that you will safely get out. There is always a chance that the hose can be looped in another direction or piled up inside the structure like spaghetti. There is also the possibility that debris could fall on the hose line and prevent you from accurately following it to the outside. But to lose the hose line in a situation such as this could be, and was, quite terrifying for these two brave men.

They made the mistake of getting separated from the hose line but did not make matters worse by splitting up. They stayed together in their quest to find a way outside without the assistance of the hose line. They had been breathing tank air for about twenty to twenty-five minutes and the low-air alarms began to vibrate. It soon turned frantic as they became disoriented and anxiety set in as they bumped off of the hallway walls in an attempt to feel for an exterior door or window.

Lieutenant Jones called for a "mayday" on his portable radio. A mayday is a fire department distress call, similar to an S.O.S. When this happens, everybody available has a new priority, the rescue of their brother firefighters. Firefighters will kick it into a higher gear, regardless of how fatigued they are, and do everything possible to assist the lost, trapped, or injured firefighters.

Other firefighters who were assisting with shagging the line for Jones and Worley were, without explanation, nowhere near them to assist. This was another major mistake, because our standard operating procedure for fire attack calls for one firefighter on the nozzle of the hose line, backed up by an officer, and then further backed up by another firefighter. In a long hose layout such as this one, a fourth firefighter is needed, if available. In this case the backup firefighter to the officer was not right behind the officer where he should have been. This was one of many things that went wrong at this incident and led to re-thinking our fire ground tactics and re-identifying our need for additional training in various areas.

The anxiety grew more and more intense as the two lost firefighters continued, unsuccessfully, to try to find a way out of the smoke that was so thick now that they couldn't see anything. They did their best to keep their composure, which was no easy feat at this juncture. They found a door to an apartment but it was locked. Firefighter Worley attempted to "mule kick" the apartment door in but was unable to compromise the heavy-duty steel. The dead bolt held it firmly in place. As hope was growing dimmer they happened upon a second door that they initially thought was another apartment. Like a gift from God they turned the knob and easily opened the unlocked door to the rear exterior staircase.

As they exited the smoke-filled hallway and into the exterior stairwell landing, the emotions that they were experiencing poured out of their bodies like free-flowing water from a spigot. They stared at each other in disbelief and, without verbalizing their thoughts, both men realized just how close they had come to dying and how unbelievably lucky they were to find the rear stairwell door in a building that they were unfamiliar with, in zero visibility, under extremely high heat conditions. They were mentally and physically exhausted, having been pushed beyond the point of fatigue.

As they walked down the stairs, the cold December air never felt more refreshing and, with each breath, the feeling of being alive was more and more comforting. They knew that they had just cheated death and it brought about mixed emotions to them. They were too tired to be ecstatic but inside they were very happy to be alive. It is probably more accurate to say they felt relieved, as opposed to happy, that they made it out. The thoughts that they also had, and will have for the rest of their lives, are the "what ifs?" These are the questions that will pop up in their minds when they least expect it. What if we hadn't found the rear stairwell door? What would we have done? Were there any other options? Would we have run out of air and died by smoke inhalation? Would our bodies have been burned up before they were found? And… would we have radioed command to tell our families that we loved them before we died? Those are some of the thoughts that come to firefighters after a brush with death. Those are the scenarios that your mind presents to you after you went deep, got the living shit scared out of you, cheated death, and compromised your edge. The beauty of it is that they lived to tell about it.

Firefighter Worley and Lieutenant Jones walked to the front of the building and into the street to get a fresh air bottle. However, at this point there would be no more going back into this building for an interior attack. This was now a defensive fire attack and would be fought from the exterior of the building. This building was constructed with wooden floors and ceilings with no fire stops built in. There was no way possible to knock this fire down at the rate it was spreading and the limited manpower we responded with.

It is at this point when a firefighter feels defeated. In his mind he struggles with different scenarios that might have provided better results and stopped the fire. He knows now that there is no second chance, no mulligan for this fire. It is a heavy-hearted, miserable feeling when you know that you failed to get the job done inside and you can only stand back and watch this fire burn out of control, destroying good people's living quarters, personal property, pictures, and family heirlooms. Worse yet, it was December, just before Christmas!

The fire had grown rapidly in size and intensity, burning through the wooden apartment roof, upward and outward to the third floor and then through the roof. The problem with this and other older buildings is the wooden construction. Once the fire gets going, it grows in intensity very rapidly. Any fire that goes through the ceiling in a wood-framed building of that size will quickly get out of control if not immediately confined by interior crews. The fact that the attack crew came up short with the initial hose line, the confusion and strategy change due to the firefighter "Mayday" call, and the lack of manpower to get other crews to the third floor, provided the fire the headway it needed to burn out of control and force the command officer to order all firefighters out of the structure.

Most newly constructed high-rise apartment buildings are built with concrete walls, ceilings, and floors in order to contain a fire to a single apartment suite. Unlike the "towering infernos" of old, the concrete construction made a tremendous difference. This type of construction is a significant benefit for firefighters, residents, and building owners alike because the fires are almost always contained to the one suite where the fire originated.

After the firefighters were evacuated, the one-hundred-foot aerial ladder was put in service, providing a large supply of water through the nozzle to the exterior of the building. By the time the mutual aid trucks arrived from neighboring Cleveland and Cleveland Heights, the fire had grown to massive proportions, engulfing nearly the entire third floor roof area. The other cities provided two additional ladder trucks to throw heavy volumes of water on the fire. This is what is referred to as a "surround and drown" tactic in the fire service. It is pretty much exactly just that- surrounding the building with aerial ladder trucks and throwing large volumes of water on the visible flames. There is not much else a firefighter can do until the aerials are shut down.

Smoke could be seen in the early-morning Cleveland skyline for miles. Although the media sensationalizes fires of this nature and seemingly every available TV news channel provides footage, firefighters really don't like to fight this type of fire.

Shift change is normally at 8:30 A.M. and fourteen firefighters and officers from "B" shift came on to relieve the cold, wet, and exhausted "A" shifters, whose tour had been extended, now on overtime, due to this third fire of their tripleheader. They were finally released from the scene at about 10:00 A.M. B shift finally shut the aerial water pipes down at approximately 12:30 in the afternoon, seven and a half hours after the fire had started.

The two things that always stand out after a day like that are the hot coffee and the hot shower, especially the shower. There is no better time in your life when you appreciate a hot shower more than after a long, cold-weather, working fire – especially the third in a tripleheader!

But if you think the job is over after the aerial ladder pipes are shut down, you are mistaken. The overhaul work on the spot fires, hidden fires, and smoldering collapsed rubble is some of the most physically demanding work you'll ever do in the fire service. I was unfortunate enough to be working B shift that day and had the unenviable pleasure of being the officer in charge of the interior overhaul of the building. The roof to the building was about ninety-five percent gone and the suites on the third floor were approximately eighty percent destroyed. Much of what was left standing on the third floor contained hidden fire, burning embers, or smoldering roof tar. The lower floors were a total loss due to the thousands of gallons of water that had been poured onto them.

We divided the third floor into three areas, front, middle, and rear, and stretched a hose line to each location. We split into three, four-man crews to overhaul each section of the third floor. To make a long, boring story short, we busted our asses for five hours, pulling ceilings down, opening up walls with axes, and removing collapsed debris to find and extinguish hidden fires. Other than the potential collapse areas and holes in the floors, we were pretty much working in a safe area with clear visibility. I was quite proud of the firefighters who really worked hard and stayed on the job with very little rest (or complaints) until the overhaul was finished. It was amazing to me that we were not called back to this building for a rekindled fire.

At the time of this fire I was fifty years old. I am, and hopefully always will be, a "working officer." In a small fire department, it is vital that you get as many bodies as possible working during our structure fires. Over the years I've noticed that many line officers were only interested in giving orders, not in helping out. That wouldn't really be an issue if we had readily available manpower like in big cities such as our neighbor Cleveland. I prefer to help my crew during and after fire attack whenever possible. It not only helps keep the men fresh, but also helps me earn my crew member's respect. This is and has always been a very high priority to me. I honestly believe that you are only as good as the men you work with and that no officer is too good or too important to do some of the same grunt work that the firefighters are called upon to do. My philosophy as an officer is simple: "Never forget where you came from." I believe that every good line officer was also a good firefighter and every good line officer has a tremendous respect and appreciation for the firefighters with whom he works.

After finishing the overhauling and leaving the Rockefeller building, we were all extremely tired. Thankfully, we did not have any more fires that day because my old bones would have been dragging. It took me two full days to recover from that fire and it reinforced my realization that firefighting is a young man's job. In fact, the profession is set up so that firefighters are able to retire at the age of 48 as long as they have completed 25 years of service. Since I started my career at age 31, I would be eligible to retire at age 56.

I made a conscious decision right then and there that I would do everything I could conceivably do to get myself in the best physical condition possible for a man my age. This was somewhat of an epiphany for me and really got me motivated. I started and remained dedicated to a rigorous exercise program and got myself in really good shape. I felt stronger, had more energy, and my mind was sharper. It gave me a renewed confidence in my ability to effectively do this job, hopefully until the day I retire.

Oh, and one more thing: On the golf course I gained an additional ten yards on my driving distance and increased my endurance. You see, for many firefighters, there is a parallel between golf and firefighting. The parallel at this stage of my career for me was to get through the firefighting years safely in order to be able to increase the golf time in retirement! And, the chances of dying on the golf course are much slimmer, that is, unless lightning strikes! And that's a risk I am more than willing to take.

> *Jerry Jones East Cleveland Firefighter to another East Cleveland firefighter after a heated argument: "Man, are you ignorant or just stupid?"*

CHAPTER 23

Fire Chief

When I was a young boy, firemen used to come to our school and talk to the children about fire safety. They were usually quite engaging and able to hold our attention. At the end of their presentation they would pass out the precious "Junior Fire Marshall" plastic badges or the red plastic fire helmets that the kids, especially the boys, cherished so much. They would put the plastic helmet on your head and say, "Look, now you're the Fire Chief."

Even as young children we were aware that the fire chief was the big boss at the firehouse. In my mind, being the fire chief was the ultimate goal for anyone who was a fireman. As a child I was quite sure that being the Fire Chief would be the best job possible for any fireman. But then I became a firefighter and found out differently.

In most full-time fire departments, the Fire Chief worked through the ranks as a firefighter and during the course of his career was promoted to lieutenant, captain, and then deputy, battalion, or assistant chief, then finally to fire chief. Until they became the chief they were always a part of the local union along with the rest of the firefighters and officers. But then, when you reach the pinnacle as fire chief, a funny thing happens. You go to "the other side!"

As the fire chief you are no longer a part of the same union that the rest of the department is. You now work directly for the city and report to the mayor. Maybe it's just me, but that never made good sense. This instantly creates a separation and drives a wedge between the chief and pretty much everybody else. I always thought that if the fire chief was still a part of our collective bargaining unit, then the relationship between the chief and the rest of the department would be much better and, as a result, more productive. On the other hand, the mayor would have a hard time buying into that line of thinking because he would lose his control over the fire chief. In East Cleveland, the chief is somewhat of a puppet for the mayor.

It does, however, explain the transformation that takes place when one is promoted to fire chief. When I saw what happened to most of the firefighters who were promoted to fire chief I knew, early on, that the job was not for me.

I saw guys get promoted to fire chief and change, almost overnight. Guys who used to have the best interests of the firefighters at heart now were the ones who were trying to put the screws to them. Some of the veteran firefighters used to joke about the transformation. They would refer to the chief's office as the "star chamber" and would say that when newly promoted chiefs walked through that door, they lost their damn minds. During my career there were seven fire chiefs, some of whom were acting chiefs and some were permanently promoted. Not all, but most of them, lost their minds when they walked into the star chamber. Their egos grew immensely with the new sense of power.

The fire chief has a juggling act to perform. He has to find a balance between handling his responsibility to manage the department and keeping costs in line with the budget. He also has to try to provide his firefighters with the best available equipment. A Fire Chief also needs to be fair and not show preferential treatment. Fire chiefs aren't always well liked, but, at least if they were good on the fire ground and at the emergency scene as a firefighter or line officer, they would be respected.

In East Cleveland, most of our Chiefs were respected for their past performance at the fire scene during their careers. Some were liked by the firefighters and some were not. Some showed preferential treatment and some did not. I can only think of one chief who was not respected or liked by almost everyone in the department. As a matter of fact, some firefighters and officers despised this guy. This chief played favorites and gave them preferential treatment. Funny, even the guys he gave preferential treatment to didn't like him. They played him, making him think they liked him, but deep down they didn't care for him. It was obvious to everyone and it did not sit well with the firefighters. He was accused of manipulating the overtime rotation to benefit his favorites, as well as himself. This is the worst kind of fire chief possible for morale building within the department. It was like a cancer spreading within our firehouse walls. This chief had a "vote of no confidence" petition brought up against him at a union meeting. He was the same guy who, as a firefighter, barely passed his probationary period even though the Fire Chief at the time encouraged his officers to give him a poor evaluation so he could fire him. This Chief was not respected or well thought of as a firefighter, line officer, or command officer. This Chief was the same guy who, as a firefighter, had rotten raw fish put into his fire gear, gloves, and boots by other firefighters who were trying to send him a message for not being a team player. This Chief was the same guy who, as a firefighter, had dead cockroaches put in his bed by other firefighters to send him a message for not being a team player. There were a few other things that firefighters did to this guy but are too foul to mention. All of these things were done to him in an effort to sway him into being a team player, to being "one of the guys". He stated, early on in his career, that "I did not get to be number one by being one of the guys!" Unfortunately, he stood by those words for his entire career. I will say this for him though, he was a good test taker, and that is why he was continually promoted.

The fire department is a team. When a new recruit takes an entrance examination, the test is always geared toward being a team player as opposed to being a loner. The goal of a fire department is to weed out people who can't work as a team within the confines of the fire house and, especially, at the emergency scene where our lives sometime depend upon the person next to you. Sometimes, however, you get loners who slip through the cracks for whatever reason may be. It's a shame when you have the head of the entire department consistently preferring disciplinary charges against firefighters and officers in an effort to make them forfeit vacation days and improve his bottom line. It's also a shame that this Fire Chief attempted on numerous occasions to mandate that firefighters pay for equipment or apparatus that were damaged during the normal course of business and firefighters were forced to go to arbitration or hire attorneys to protect their rights. He had no problem writing guys up on petty disciplinary charges but didn't always visit injured firefighters at Huron Hospital, only a couple minutes away from the engine house. He also had a very difficult time commending the firefighters for bravery or lifesaving emergencies. This guy was on his own little island and was definitely one of the few who "slipped through the cracks!"

Fortunately, fire chiefs come and go. During my career there were seven chiefs in 26 years. The Chiefs' tenure is often short because they move into that rank toward the end of their career. A fire department should be proud of their Chief, not embarrassed by him. A Fire Chief should be there for the firefighters even though he reports to the Mayor. Good, fair-minded Fire Chiefs are able to achieve the balance necessary to manage the budget and keep the members of the department motivated. The Chief is responsible for the morale of the department. If the morale is low, then the motivation will be lacking and will sometimes affect job performance. It starts at the top with the Fire Chief. It seems that sometimes the Chief is stuck between a rock and a hard place but that's what you will get when you pass through that door and enter into the star chamber.

East Cleveland veteran firefighter to new recruit: "Go down to the basement and get me the board stretcher. It's right next to the bubble pump for the level!"

CHAPTER 24

Rumors

I'll never forget when I heard a sweet elderly lady remark that she thought all firefighters were honest, trustworthy, and good role models for young kids. Although there is a certain amount of truth to that statement, by no means are all firefighters squeaky clean. In fact, over the years, there have been some "bad boys" who have come and gone through the firehouse doors. We had our share of thrill seekers and guys who didn't follow all of the rules. I had the dubious honor of working with some of these guys. I was also fortunate enough to hear about some of the characters who came before me from the old timers.

It's true that firefighters have a lot of down time and sometimes boredom sets in. Their minds often wander and they think of some outrageous things to do to pass the time. There are also some guys who are a little bit nuts to begin with. After all, you have to be a little bit nuts to run into a burning building. I am going to pass on some of the stories about some of the crazy firefighters who have worked in East Cleveland over the past thirty to forty years. No names will be attached to the characters in these stories in order to protect the guilty.

Drinking alcohol while on duty is both prohibited and unwise in the fire service. It's a serious rules infraction that can get you fired. Even though the consequences are severe if one gets caught drinking on duty, there are rumors that firefighters did, occasionally, drink while on duty. One instance comes to mind about firefighters drinking on duty on the same day that a fire occurred. The fire was at an apartment building and night club at Lakeview and Euclid avenues.

The alarm for the fire came in at 8:30 A.M.- shift change, so two platoons were involved in the extinguishment. The building was a three-story structure with a mixed occupancy, with sixteen apartments on the upper floors and a nightclub and retail space on the first floor. The fire got a very good head start and had penetrated multiple floors upon our arrival. The firefighters went inside and fought this fire to the best of their ability. It was one of those fires that had to be chased all over the many avenues of fire travel that were a part of this structure. This was a very dangerous fire and we were extremely lucky that nobody was seriously hurt or killed. Three firefighters fell partially through the floor due to fires burning underneath them and weakening the wood structural members. One firefighter lost his helmet and it fell into a sea of flames underneath him. I can remember going into a sub-basement with two other firefighters about forty-five minutes into the fire. It was like hell in there. There was fire in every direction and the ceiling was falling all around us. I could see and hear falling hot embers dropping all over the room. I just knew that there was going to be a collapse and we would die. Luckily, we got out of the basement in time. But we stayed in there too long and when we left, it was still burning intensely. It had gotten to the point where no small hose lines were going to put out this fast-moving fire.

We had an inexperienced command officer and he did not get the men out in a timely fashion. We stayed in too long and had firefighters scattered all over this building attempting to stop the spread of flames. After over an hour of interior firefighting, this fire was raging worse than when we arrived.

I was a team leader that day, in charge of a four-man crew. At this point I was on the second floor where two hose lines were deployed. They were fully opened but the fire was so intense that they were not doing much good. Sections of ceiling were falling all around us and you could hear the fire roaring everywhere. I knew that we had to get out, so I went outside to check the exterior and confer with the O.I.C.

I took one look at the exterior and I could tell that the fire was about to break through the roof. I didn't realize it at the time, but melted tar had fallen onto the top of my helmet and it was smoking as I approached our O.I.C. I looked him directly in the eyes and said, "You have got to pull everyone out, now!" It is not safe inside!" He looked like a deer in the headlights and did not respond. I repeated, "Get everyone out, now!" He looked right past me as if I didn't exist. I don't know if it was because I was just a team leader and not an officer, or if it was because he really didn't know what to do. Regardless, he wouldn't make the call to evacuate the building. I turned to look at the building and as I did a massive ball of fire broke through the roof. This fire was completely out of control!

Firefighter Rick Razek, who had witnessed my plea to get the men out, took it on his own accord and went over to the fire engine and sounded the air horns distress signal, three short blasts of the air horns sounded repeatedly, letting all firefighters inside the structure know that interior firefighting operations were halted and we would now employ defensive exterior operations. When the air horns sound, all firefighters are supposed to immediately cease all activity, exit the structure, and report to the outside command center for a personnel accountability report.

All firefighters exited the building safely, some coming out after a few minutes, providing everyone some anxious moments. The firefighters were physically and mentally exhausted and beaten down. The fire had broken through the roof, but not without one hell of an effort by about twenty-five guys who really stayed inside too long. The O.I.C. almost got guys hurt by waiting too long. If not for Razek sounding the air horns without being ordered to do so, who knows what might have transpired.

Normally a firefighter is only supposed to sound the air horns when ordered to do so by the O.I.C. On this day that didn't happen. The firefighter did the right thing and was not disciplined. The O.I.C. didn't say anything to him because he knew that he, himself, had screwed up. Looking back, the O.I.C. should have been written up for jeopardizing the safety of firefighters and not listening to his interior people. I should have pursued this but did not. I gave the O.I.C. the benefit of the doubt because he was new and inexperienced in the role of command officer.

The most important thing was that all of the firefighters got out of the building safely. We were very lucky that day, escaping multiple incidents where guys really could have been injured. The bottom line was that we stayed inside too long, didn't save the property, and almost got firefighters killed. The exterior firefighting operations lasted for a couple hours, with aerial ladder trucks pouring thousands of gallons of water onto the burning rubble. The building was a total loss. The firefighters rested during exterior operations until they shut down the aerials and interior overhaul commenced. This is often the most physically demanding aspect of the job because much of the structure is collapsed and there are numerous pockets of small fires that need to be extinguished. This is no small task when already exhausted firefighters are called on to move this extremely heavy smoldering rubble.

You may be wondering, what does any of this have to do with drinking on the job? Well, rumor had it that the firefighters set up two rehab areas inside the building during the overhaul operations. It was said that an apartment on the second floor was still intact and had almost a full case of cold beer in the refrigerator. Supposedly the firefighters took short refreshment breaks there to replenish fluids. I heard one firefighter say that he was so thirsty that he drank a can of beer in about ten seconds. I can't substantiate this rumor, but I do remember seeing a whole lot of empty beer cans on the floor of this apartment.

Rumor has it that the other rehab area was at the opposite end of the building on the first floor. This just happened to be the location of the 30/30 Nightclub. I never made it down to this rehab area, but I heard that the fluids that were replenished here were not just beer. After it was all said and done, everyone left the scene with a second wind and sheepish grins on their faces. I had heard from the old timers that a beer never tasted so good as it does right after a tough working fire. I guess they were right. At least that was what the rumor was!

Although our rules and regulations state that no weapons are allowed in the engine house, rumor has it that some guys decided to break that rule. Supposedly a group of guys on "A" shift decided that they were going to use a water balloon launcher to fire from the roof of fire station number one to the houses, cars, pedestrians, and businesses that surround the fire station.

They made a giant slingshot that required three people to launch. The balloons would fly tremendous distances, hanging in the air for almost five seconds. Their targets ranged from random houses, public transit busses, cars and people on Euclid Avenue, and the Rally's fast food restaurant across the street from city hall. They were launched so far that the unsuspecting victims had no idea whatsoever where they were coming from.

The water balloon launcher was a huge success, with the culmination being when they busted one on the windows of a bus and another one on a car that was in line for the drive thru at Rally's. It reminded me of a bunch of college students fooling around and having a "giggle fest" at a fraternity house. I must admit that it was pretty amusing. The balloon launching was short-lived. This was a good thing because nobody got hurt and they would most likely have eventually been caught and disciplined.

There could be a legitimate argument over whether or not a balloon launcher is actually a weapon. There is, however, no argument that a 44-caliber pistol and an Uzi submachine gun are weapons. Rumor has it that a firefighter brought a 44 Magnum handgun into the engine house one weekend. He snuck up to the roof of fire station number one with a couple of other guys when the officer in charge was out of the engine house on a detail. He told the other firefighters that he was going to put a bullet into the clock tower at Kirk Junior High School, which was located about a tenth of a mile up Marloes Avenue. True to his word, this firefighter, who I will refer to as "Pork Pig," fired a couple shots from the pistol toward the clock tower. It was never confirmed whether he hit his target. Luckily for Pork Pig, he never got caught. Gunfire, you see, was a noise that is heard on a fairly regular basis in East Cleveland. It's not uncommon to hear shots fired right next to the police station, as was done on that day by Firefighter Pork Pig!

To piggyback on the Pork Pig story is another weapon rumor, this time with an Uzi submachine gun owned by another firefighter whom I will refer to as "The Brick." It was New Year's Eve and it was a well-known fact that the citizens of East Cleveland celebrate the New Year at midnight with firearms instead of fireworks. Don't get me wrong, some people also shoot off fireworks, but the majority of the noise you hear is gunfire. It's insane! It's like a war zone at midnight! You will hear every kind of gun blast imaginable, including pistols, rifles, shotguns, and machine guns. There was an unwritten rule that the police and firefighters do their best to stay in quarters from midnight until about 12:15 am. We used to take a tape recorder onto the rooftop at fire station number one to record the gunfire. It was incredible, especially the first time that you hear it. It seems as if half of the population is firing off rounds.

On this particular New Year's Eve, I was surprised by "The Brick." At about two minutes before midnight, he walked into the lounge and called to me very nonchalantly, then waved me to the rear of the engine house. Keep in mind that the police station is right next door and almost all of the police cruisers are parked in the rear parking lot that they share with all other city employees. "The Brick" reached into a large brown paper bag and pulled out a fully loaded Uzi submachine gun. He looked at me and said, "Watch this shit, Mike."

I couldn't believe it. He walked right out through the back door into the parking lot and emptied out the Uzi. It was actually an awesome, impressive display of firepower, but I couldn't believe that he had the stones to do it in the parking lot. It blended in with the thousands of other guns that were blasting away. There were so many bullets flying that you could actually hear an occasional slug fall harmlessly to the ground of the parking lot. The important thing was to stay low or under cover for at least ten minutes.

The Brick pulled it off without getting into any trouble or anyone getting hurt. As I returned to the fire department lounge I thought about what had just transpired and again I said to myself, "Only in East Cleveland!"

Then there was the rumor about the creepers! The creepers were the guys who would take a portable radio with them then go on nightly "details." The creepers were the guys with a very high sex drive who couldn't keep it in their pants for a twenty-four-hour shift. These were the guys who thought about sex more often than not. There was one guy, in particular, who was a sex maniac. One day he pulled a shopping bag full of women's panties out of his locker. No, he wasn't a cross dresser. The panties were from all of the girls he had been with. These panties were symbols of his conquests. He was like the gunfighter who put notches on his belt for every kill that he made, only his notches were women's panties. He liked the "thick" girls too, as evidenced by some of the extra-large panties in the bag.

He was like a dog in heat. He sized up every woman he laid eyes on and immediately imagined himself in bed with her. He would approach them anywhere, and at any time. To him, rejection meant only to try again or move on to the next one. He brought girls into the engine house late at night with only one thing on his mind. He had sex with these girls in every imaginable place – the parking lots, the dorm, the bathrooms, the basement, the tunnel, the lounge, the officer's room at station number two, the kitchen, and of course he had to do it on top of the hose bed on the fire engine like they did in the movie Backdraft. He was just a "dog," flat out!

There were other creepers too. Most were more discreet, but they had the same goal in mind. More than one guy had two or three girlfriends at the same time. They would continually lie to and deceive these girls to keep them from discovering their transgressions. It was like a big game to them and they really had to work hard at it to keep from being found out. Other firefighters were asked to lie if anyone called for them at work and tell them that they were out on an alarm or detail. Some guys would do it, but others didn't care to get caught up in the lies. There were a few times when a creeper had one girlfriend going out the back door at station number one and another one coming in the front door. It was crazy! It seemed like the creepers had many close calls and most were eventually caught or, at least, under suspicion. I honestly believe that the creepers did it not only for the sex, but also for the adrenaline rush that came with the possibility of getting caught.

Another rumor that originated during the administration of an iron-fisted mayor had to do with firefighters cutting grass. This mayor said that he would get "those lazy suckas out of those Lazy Boy chairs and make them cut some grass." This one made the national news and traveled across the Internet pipeline in a New York minute.

He portrayed the East Cleveland firefighters as lazy and greedy individuals who "stole" overtime dollars from the taxpayers. We butted heads with this administration from day one and they made every effort to blast us in the media and turn the citizens against us. As far as cutting the grass, he did, in fact, make firefighters cut grass when on duty. Forget the fact that we ran between five thousand to six thousand EMS and fire alarms per year with only twelve firefighters and officers. He still tried to convince the citizens that we were lazy. He even stated that our jobs were no more dangerous than his secretary's. So, he ordered the firefighters to cut grass during their twenty-four-hour shifts.

Rumor has it that when one of the firefighters was cutting grass on a very expensive heavy-duty mower, he ran it into a huge rock that was hidden under some high grass. Unfortunately, the rock caused major damage to the mower and rendered it useless. Inquiring minds wanted to know if the firefighter ran over the rock on purpose. As of now the answer is no, but only he knows for sure. That incident, along with public outcry and some of the mayor's peers who ridiculed his decision to have firefighters cut grass while on duty, ended the grass-cutting for the firefighters. Instead of saving the taxpayers money, it ended up costing them money to repair the broken lawnmower.

There was another rumor from the time of the same administration that can now be validated. City hall ordered the firefighters to pass out, door to door, ten thousand flyers with the mayor's photograph attached, promoting a new tax amnesty program. The firefighters felt that he was being vindictive because of all our grievances and court actions against the city (the court sided with us on all of them). He ordered the firefighters, but no other city employees, to handle this monumental task along with our other regular duties. The firefighters took exception to this and approximately nine thousand of the flyers came up missing after a couple days. The mayor was incensed and ordered an investigation and threatened to fire those involved. To make a long story short, the Mayor lost his re-election bid shortly after "Flyer gate" and what once was a rumor can now be confirmed: The flyers got tossed in the dumpster, all nine thousand of them. Don't mess with ECFD!

And then there was the fire watch. None of the firefighters involved will ever forget the cash cow at a high rise building in East Cleveland. Due to an electrical fire that resulted in five floors being taken out of service, the property was put on a fire watch until power was restored and the fire alarm system was back up and running.

This fire watch was a sweetheart deal for the firefighters. For $33.00 per hour, we were expected to walk all twenty-seven floors every hour, twenty-four hours a day, seven days a week. Guys signed up for eight-hour shifts, and two firefighters worked (and I use this term loosely) together during each shift. An apartment efficiency suite on the first floor served as the headquarters for the duration of the fire watch. The suite was furnished with a couch, table, chairs, TV, and refrigerator. There was a separate bedroom with a double bed and bathroom. Pretty much all of the creature comforts that were needed to help complete this "difficult" task, were included.

At the beginning of the fire watch, the firefighters walked the floors as instructed, every hour, 24/7, making sure that nothing was on fire. Shortly after the watch was initiated, the fire alarm system was restored to all but the five floors that were damaged during the fire. Realistically there only needed to be a fire watch for those five floors. One person could have handled this detail and it could have been an employee of the building owner at, say, $8 per hour. For some unknown reason, the property manager made no effort to remove the firefighters from the fire watch and replace us with his own people. Who were we to tell the property manager to stop throwing money at us? The East Cleveland mayor was quoted as saying " the firefighters fire watch is like Butch and Sundance robbing the train" Not only did the property manager leave us on the job, but he also let the detail drag on for more than six months, until the alarm system was fully restored to the entire building.

There was a rumor that when the alarm system was restored to all but five floors, the fire watch procedure changed drastically. To this day the rumor cannot be substantiated, but it came from numerous reliable sources who refused to name names. Rumor has it that some firefighters stopped walking twenty-two of the twenty-seven floors and only walked five floors. After a while the rumor was that they only walked the five floors twice per shift, during the first hour and the last. Rumor has it that some guys came in, signed the time sheet and went to sleep. Eight hours later they would wake up and go home, not once walking the floors.

There were other unsubstantiated rumors that circulated in regard to the fire watch. Rumor had it that some guys came to the fire watch drunk then passed out shortly after arriving for their shift. Rumor has it that some guys would have their partner sign them in then arrive a couple hours late. They, in turn, would return the favor for their partner at the next shift. Rumor has it that guys would bring beer in and party during their watch. Rumor has it that some guys would bring girls in and have sex with them during their watch. Finally, rumor has it that some guys took turns not even showing up for the fire watch and they were signed in by their partners who would also complete their time sheet.

It's possible that all of these rumors were true, but on the other hand, they could also be untrue. The amazing thing is that the property managers allowed the fire watch to drag on as long as they did. The alarm system could have been restored much sooner. Something didn't seem right about the building owner apparently not caring about spending ridiculous money for the fire watch. Even though the money was generated from their insurance claim, it seemed like they were in no hurry to end this thing. The final rumor pertaining to the fire watch issue was that the building owner let the fire watch go on as long as it did because they were getting more money from the insurance company than they were paying out to the firefighters. But, like the rest of the fire watch rumors, this one too could not be substantiated. So much for rumors!

Recruit firefighter, first day on the job: "Would anybody like some of this cake that my girlfriend made?"

Veteran firefighter: "Stick it up your ass but nice of you to offer."

CHAPTER 25

Promotions

In most jobs, receiving a promotion and raise in pay is a joyous occasion, a time to enjoy the rewards of your hard work and dedication. This event should be celebrated by family, friends, and co-workers. There should be no jealousy, bitterness, or complaining. It should be a time for congratulating, high-fiving, and back-slapping. But, as we know, this is not a perfect world and, throughout my career in East Cleveland, promotions have always been tainted and filled with bitterness, controversy, and manipulation.

Nobody likes to hear whining and complaining, especially from grown men or women. In the past some very good firefighters have been passed over for promotion and didn't complain much. On the other hand, you had less deserving individuals who were passed over and bitched, moaned, and bellyached to anyone who would listen. I never really liked to hear the sour grapes and complaining from people. But for the truly deserving individuals who were passed over unjustly, I really felt for them. It takes the wind out of your sail when you are wrongly passed over. It affects your motivation, attitude, and morale. It also affects your co-workers, to an extent.

It has to do with the process, and the promotion process has always been flawed in East Cleveland. I saw early on that the best people weren't always promoted. There were guys who were tremendous on the fire ground, well respected, brave, and true leaders. However, some of these individuals were never promoted because they were not good test-takers. I always thought that other criteria, in addition to written and oral examinations, should determine who advanced in rank, specifically the opinions of all of your peers and, to a lesser degree, seniority. The firefighters and other officers know who is deserving and who is not. I always thought that if every candidate for promotion was evaluated by all of his peers, then the most deserving individuals would advance. In East Cleveland, we had no such criteria and, because of our testing procedures, undeserving people slipped through the cracks and others were denied what they worked so hard for and truly deserved.

For the majority of my career, the promotion process for lieutenants and captains consisted of three steps. A list of five or six books pertaining to the fire service was issued and candidates were usually given two to three months to study them. A written examination and a skills assessment center were the first two steps. An assessment center will present written and oral emergency scene scenarios to the candidates who are asked to explain how they would handle them as a promoted officer. An oral interview with experienced, impartial fire service officers (generally chiefs and captains) would be the final hurdle in the process. After these three events, the scores were tallied and the candidates were ranked. Although this process didn't always get the best qualified individuals, at least it was thorough and you had to know a lot about the fire service and our department. It was a bit flawed but, at the same time, it was very comprehensive.

The problems would arise after the promotional list was certified. For instance, Frank Malinowski, a guy who came on the department the same year I did, scored second on the lieutenant's exam but was passed over by the fire chief a few times in order for him to be able to promote his college fraternity brother, who was ranked sixth. Frank was a white man who was well liked and respected by all of the firefighters, both black and white. He had no enemies on the department. He was a God-fearing family man. He was smart, good natured, reliable, loyal, and one hell of a firefighter. Frank was laid back and didn't complain. He didn't call off sick. He just came in every day and did a great job. He was an asset to the department and a great guy to have by your side at the emergency scene. But because Frank wasn't a complainer, the chief decided that he would be the guy to get passed over in order to promote his fraternity brother.

Frank, true to his nature, quietly accepted his fate. And there really was no guarantee that had he pissed, moaned, and complained, it would have changed the outcome. In the process he was a victim of the worst travesty of justice to any East Cleveland firefighter in a promotional exam that ever occurred. Some firefighters also viewed this action as racist because the chief was black, as was the man he promoted over Frank.

In the end, the East Cleveland Fire Department was the loser. Frank's spirit was broken but it didn't stop him from continuing to come to work and do the great job that he had always done, at least until he found a way out. Frank ended up taking a job from another department, and their gain was our loss. I am quite sure that he would not have left our department had he not been screwed so badly. Even though I was not the one who was passed over, I felt the sting because he was my friend, my Bunkie, and it was just plain wrong! I felt the sting but only Frank knew exactly how miserable it felt. Funny thing, though, near the end of my career I also felt the sting, but this time I felt it firsthand.

I too was passed over, but for the rank of captain. I did not plan to write about this unpleasant event and sound like a complainer because, in the past, that turned me off when others did. However, I want this book to be an honest appraisal of what can, and does, occur in the career of a firefighter. I need to tell this story because it was a monumental event in my career, even though it was a low point and I would honestly like to forget all about it. I have decided to present only the facts, without complaints or a "woe is me" attitude attached to them. I will keep my opinions to a minimum and, from there, let the chips fall where they may. Readers can form their own opinions.

A fire captain's promotional examination was announced. But this particular examination process would be unlike all previous captain's promotional tests ever administered during my then-twenty-three years on the department. When the fire chief was asked which books we would have to study for the test, he said none because there would be no written test. Nor would there be a skills assessment center. There was only to be a 10-minute oral interview with three "impartial monitors."

This drastic change in the examination process made many firefighters, and not just the candidates, think that the fix was in. Even before this examination was given, there was a standing joke in the engine house that if you weren't a "W" then you weren't getting promoted. This was a reference to three of the black lieutenants whose first or last names began with a "W."

Regarding the "impartial monitors": On the day of the examination, one of the monitors did not show up. Although I later made several attempts to find out who this third person was and why they did not show up, nobody in the city administration could provide me that answer. I still find this very peculiar. But the examination proceeded anyway with only two monitors. Both of these monitors were black men. Only one of these men had fire service experience. He was a battalion chief for the City of Cleveland. He was also a three-time past president of the International Association of Black Professional Firefighters and he personally knew some of the black lieutenants who were taking this examination. The other monitor was a civil service commission member with no actual firefighting experience.

There were eight lieutenants taking this examination, and four were black and four were white. Keep in mind that the citizen population, and the city administration was almost one hundred percent black. Each candidate was asked ten generic fire service-related questions, then graded by both monitors on their responses. When it was all said and done, the black lieutenants were ranked first, second, third and fifth. I was ranked fourth and the other white lieutenants finished sixth, seventh and eighth. From this list, four lieutenants were promoted to Captain. All of the black lieutenants were promoted, even the one who finished fifth, behind me.

I was very angry about being passed over, but more so because of the way the entire process went down. It was never personal for me with any of the black guys who were promoted. I liked and respected all of them. Still do. They were all good, solid people. They were all capable of becoming excellent captains. None of them were malcontents or screw ups. As a matter of fact, the lieutenant who was in the fifth position approached me after he was promoted ahead of me. He said that we always got along and worked together well and that he didn't want this to affect our relationship. He said he would understand if I challenged this and to go ahead and "do what you gotta do." I assured him that there was no way it would affect our relationship because it was not personal with him or the others. I will always respect him for being a man and saying that to me, face to face.

All eight of the lieutenants who took the examination were damn good line officers and leaders. I was more upset about the process and how our fire chief was able to pull this whole thing off. I had a very good reputation on the fire ground and in the engine house. If I was a screw up, I would understand being passed over. From an experience standpoint, I had nine to ten years more experience as a lieutenant than three of the promoted lieutenants. I also had a couple years' experience as an acting captain and they had none. I even had my own platoon for six months. At the end of the day, none of that counted, and it stung bad! I had wanted so badly to be a command-level officer at the end of my career and I truly believed that I was deserving. Not to mention the lost wages and lower pension, as a result.

But the last thing that I wanted to do at this point in my career was challenge being passed over to captain. As you get older, you learn to choose your battles. You learn that most of these battles aren't worth the effort. But I believed that the process was so obviously discriminatory that I had to fight it. I really wasn't sure how to fight it, but I decided that it had to be done.

I ended up consulting with our union attorney as well as my own personal attorney. I was advised to file a complaint through the Ohio Civil Rights Commission. I did this and, after a few months, the final decision was in favor of the city administration, due largely to some statute of limitations within the Civil Rights Commission as well as some city ordinances that were in place which allowed them to conduct this type of promotional exam.

I was not surprised by the decision and I knew that my best chance for justice was in a court of law. At this point I was pretty tired of fighting. I really didn't want any part of this from the beginning. I decided to let it go and move on. I didn't know exactly what my chances would have been in the court system, but I needed to move on and let go of the anger. What I thought was obvious discrimination turned out to be hard to prove. Maybe I should have continued to fight, but I chose to do my remaining time then ride off into the sunset.

I know that a lot of negative things happened over the years during some of the promotions, but also that you can't hold onto anger and negativity. I know that I had a great job and most of the time things were very positive. I moved on and was content to finish my career as a lieutenant for the East Cleveland Fire Department. I still firmly believe in the brotherhood of this department and I am proud to be a part of it. I didn't want to create a gap between myself and the black firefighters because I have always gotten along great with them. I believe that most of these guys understood why I challenged the promotional.

This will be the last time I discuss these negative events. I am back to enjoying this job that I truly love. I focus on the positives. I will try not to let anyone steal my joy. I will strongly recommend this career to any young man or woman who shows an interest. I realize that you only have so much time on this Earth and I prefer to have fun and be happy. I thank God every day for all that I have and try to remember that "every day on the right side of the dirt is a good day!"

> "Is someone back there? Ya there's someone back there."
>
> (Firefighter Mick Gunn talking in his sleep)

CHAPTER 26

Circling the Drain

The phrase "circling the drain" is used in East Cleveland to describe some of the veteran firefighters and officers who were at or near the end of their careers. It refers, jokingly, to guys staying employed after they are eligible to retire. The guys who are using the phrase would love to see the veterans retire so they can move up on the seniority list. However, nowadays there are a few factors to consider when one is at or near retirement age. One is the outrageous cost of health insurance. Another is the cost of a college education. Many guys near retirement age have kids in college at that stage of their lives. All of these things are taken into consideration when a guy is entertaining the idea of retiring.

In the state of Ohio, in order for a firefighter to retire, he must meet two criteria. He must be fifty-two years of age or older, and have at least twenty-five years of service. So, anyone starting in the fire service at age twenty-seven or younger has the option to retire at fifty-two. There are not very many other jobs available where a person can retire so young.

The skyrocketing rise in health care premiums in the late 1990s and early 2000s kept many firefighters working who may have otherwise chosen retirement. Some of the retirees who, as active firefighters, paid very low or no monthly health care premiums, are now paying $600 to $800 per month, and sometimes more, for medical health benefits. Some firefighters literally couldn't afford to retire because of this cost. Many people in the general public had the misconception that all retired firefighters were able to receive great medical benefits at little or no cost to them. That was the case for many years but has since changed drastically, most likely forever.

The significant rise in college tuition, room and board, along with the cost of health care premiums, also kept many firefighters on the job longer than they'd anticipated. These were initially the main factors that needed to be taken into consideration by firefighters. That is, until the advent of the DROP (Deferred Retirement Option Program). This program kept many guys circling the drain, and for thousands of good reasons!

The DROP program was initiated in 2003. The program is an optional benefit that allows eligible police officers and firefighters to accumulate a sizable lump sum of money for retirement. The person retires, on paper, but continues to work at their current wage. Their pension amount is calculated and frozen. The monies that were going into the pension fund now go into the DROP. After some nice compound interest, participants are able to accumulate lump sum amounts averaging anywhere from $100,000 to more than $500,000, depending on their salary, years of service at the date of retirement, and years in the DROP program. To participate in the program without penalty, one must remain in the program for a minimum of five years and up to a maximum of eight years. Firefighters are now continuing to work up to eight years longer and the result for them is a substantial monetary benefit. There are, however, some concerns about firefighters staying too long.

A firefighter will normally rotate into a job that is suitable for him as he nears retirement age. By this time, he may be an officer or will have enough seniority and experience to be able to land a position such as fire inspector, dispatcher, or apparatus engineer. Let's face it, firefighting is a young man's job. Not many people will dispute that. Fighting fires takes a toll on your body and not all firefighters over the age of fifty are physically fit enough to carry out this task. I believe in taking care of the firefighters who are at or near the end of their careers. However, in East Cleveland and many other smaller fire departments, there aren't many positions available for guys who can't fight fires anymore. Unless you are a shift O.I.C. or an apparatus driver, you will be going into and working at the fire scene. There really is no place to hide. Even the drivers are called upon to help out at some of the more intense working fires.

Because some firefighters are continuing to work well into their late fifties and sometimes even their sixties, there is a legitimate concern for them if they are on the front lines or leading crews inside as line officers. This is where it gets to be a bit complicated. Plain and simple, some guys just can't do it anymore and should not be going into fires. Sure, you want to take care of the guys who have paid their dues for more than twenty-five years, but in no way should you do so if it compromises the effectiveness or safety of the other firefighters.

The responsibility to know when to retire falls on those who are eligible. They should realize when they can no longer do the job and be content taking a position that doesn't jeopardize others. In fact, firefighters are very fortunate that they are able to be protected as they near retirement because if they were forced to retire before they are ready, it would very often have an adverse effect on them and their families.

The mindset of a firefighter who is nearing his retirement date is, as expected, quite different from the new recruit. The new recruits are usually extremely eager for knowledge and have a burning desire to fight fires, regardless of the time of day, weather conditions, or how fatigued they are at the time. They just want fires and the adrenaline rush that comes with going inside and "slaying the red devil." It could be four in the morning with below-zero temperatures outside and some new guys are still glad to catch a fire. To them, it's almost like performing in a team sporting event or a mini-war. "It's game day!" "It's show time!" The combatants pour their hearts and souls out on the battlefield in order to win, or in our case, to extinguish the flames. When the battle is over there is an overwhelming feeling of satisfaction in the victory over the fire. The firefighters feel good knowing that they flirted with danger and came out on top. They rehash the details of the fire and what part each played in its extinguishment. This will go on shortly after the fire is out and will continue for a few days, eventually dying down until it has been discussed with the other shifts as well. Finally, the events of the fire will end up as another war story conversation piece that will come up occasionally when the firefighters who were involved look back and reminisce.

The enthusiasm displayed by the young guys is infectious and helps keep the veterans motivated. It reminds the vets of how they were years ago and gives them an incentive to dig deep and hang in there with the younger, stronger, more physically fit firefighters. Although most of the veterans are nowhere near as fit as the young guys, they have much more knowledge and experience. This helps them fight a fire smarter instead of harder and expend less energy. Over the years the vets have learned how to pace themselves and control their breathing under duress and anxious moments. They are the calm, cool, and collected firefighters who take a little extra time to size up a situation, think it through, then employ their tactics in a systematic manner.

A new firefighter has more of a tendency to charge in, with wide-eyed reckless abandon, without considering all of the things that could go wrong. The young guys quickly understand that the veterans have a wealth of experience and that they need to tap into it in order to get better. The smart young firefighters develop the proper attitude to let the vets know they are worthy of this knowledge. Almost all veteran firefighters will gladly pass on their knowledge to battle-tested young firefighters who respect the traditions and the correct way to do the job. These young firefighters whom they've come to know and trust will use the knowledge wisely and pass it on to others who will come after them, thus securing the fundamentals and practices that have been in place in the fire service for many years.

Most veteran firefighters who are close to retirement will admit that they don't care if they ever have another fire. This is quite contrary to how a new recruit normally thinks. In fact, if a new recruit would say this, many would question their resolve or eagerness to be in this profession. Veteran firefighters love to hear young guys say they "hope we get a fire soon."

I can remember the first time I heard a veteran firefighter say he didn't want to fight anymore fires. I was surprised and somewhat disappointed. The proven veterans, however, can get away with making that statement. They have paid their dues on countless occasions over the years. They have seen and experienced so much but they understand that they will be paid the same whether they fight a fire or do nothing. It is at this stage in their careers when most will opt to get paid to do nothing. The macho attitude of "needing" another fire is gone by the wayside, replaced now by the "let's sleep through the night" attitude. They still enjoy the rush and endorphin release that takes place during firefighting, but if they had the option, most would prefer to let the next shift fight the fires. Sure, it's satisfying to work hard and do a good job at a tough fire, but the beating your body takes and the recovery involved, makes the vets opt for fire-free days. It's the "coming full circle" and normal evolution of the recruit firefighter into the experienced veteran.

It's a career that your co-workers will tell you will go by quickly, but you won't believe them. You won't believe them at first because the time seems to go slowly then. You can't wait for the day when another new guy is hired and he is the one who is under the microscope and is constantly being evaluated. You want to get the probationary period over with because it sucks being a boot firefighter. Then, one day, you have five years on and you are settled in. Things go much smoother and your confidence level in your ability to do the job is increased. Time seems to go a bit faster. You are now into a routine and time creeps up on you. Ten, fifteen, twenty years go by, and you look back and find it hard to believe. You are glad because you are nearing retirement but, in the back of your mind, you realize that you are now the old guy, like those who you looked to for advice when you were a new recruit years ago. You also take ownership of the realization that you are much closer to taking that final "dirt nap under the Parthenon" than you've ever been. Yes, you are one step closer to death.

At this point in time, you are one of the guys who is circling the drain. You are considering the D.R.O.P. and trying to calculate your expenses in hopes that you will be financially sound in the retirement years. Many guys work other jobs in retirement. They "double dip" for a few years by working and collecting their pension.

A lot of things go through your mind at the end of your career. You think of how much has happened during your career. You think of some of the amazing things you saw and experienced over the years. You think of your first day on the job and you can't believe that it's almost over. You think of the day when you will get "blown out" – when, at 8:30 A.M., all of the East Cleveland fire apparatus line Marloes Avenue outside of station number one with lights on, sirens and horns blaring, and you walk out into the street where a sea of your brothers, active and retired firefighters, have gathered to congratulate you. It's a very emotional event at times.

Mostly you think of the people you worked with. The memories, the war stories that will last forever. The bonds that you made are rock solid. The friends are like brothers and are for life. These are people whom you trust like family members. You've gone through so much together over the years. That is the best thing about the fire service! To be part of a team of brave, aggressive, fun-loving, down-to-earth, genuine people, and get paid to do it, is not a bad deal at all. I made the right decision when I took a $10,000 pay cut back in 1988 to come to work in East Cleveland. For me, it was an honor and a privilege to work with the best firefighters in the State of Ohio, people I love like brothers, who will carry on the traditions and reputation that make our tiny city in East Cleveland unique, quite special, and like no other!

Quotable #27: "Hey man, do you know that you have a knife stuck in your head?"

(EMT to patient- actual EMS run)

CHAPTER 27

The Blowout

I became eligible for retirement on October 10, 2013, but planned to stay a bit longer. I was fifty-six years old and in fairly good physical condition. Initially I planned on doing another three years in the D.R.O.P. to help pay for my daughter Shannon's college tuition. However, the program had changed and, in order to collect interest on the money in the D.R.O.P. account, a minimum of five years participation was now required. I knew that I wasn't going to stay five more years. Hell, three more years would have been tough. So, I decided that I would do two more years and forfeit the interest that would accrue because I wouldn't be doing the required minimum. The new goal was to retire in October of 2015 but, because of the financial condition of the city, I decided to cut that goal short as well.

The State of Ohio declared East Cleveland to be in state of fiscal distress in 1988, the year I was hired. That situation continued for 18 years. In 2007, the city government figured its way out of the mess, but ended up back in fiscal emergency in 2012. By 2014, East Cleveland had deteriorated so badly that recovery was nearly impossible. I will never understand how they were ever removed from the fiscal emergency designation by the State of Ohio. Things had steadily declined and were never really noticeably better.

Over the last few years of my career, the city's spending was supervised by a state fiscal commission. The state auditor released a report in November 2014 which said, "East Cleveland is on the verge of financial collapse after a recovery plan proved inadequate." He also said that, "the poverty-stricken suburb has been able to meet payroll thus far only through sheer luck." He further stated that, "East Cleveland's fire department doesn't have a working ladder truck, the city can no longer provide adequate street maintenance, all city cell phones have been shut off, and utility companies are threatening legal action for unpaid bills." Believe it or not, the gas was actually shut off to city hall for a day. Just when you thought it couldn't get any worse, it did!

The citizens knew that things were bad, but until that report was released, they really hadn't known just how bad. Medical bills for city employees went unpaid for months. Our fire apparatus was in dire need of upgrading but there was hardly enough money for emergency repairs and almost none for regular maintenance. There were days when we had no working ambulances and had to almost beg the surrounding communities to transport our patients to the hospital. Two neighboring suburbs refused to provide mutual aid to us because we couldn't reciprocate. Hell, we were breaking all the protocols and transporting patients in fire trucks and our command vehicle. It was embarrassing to us and a disservice to our citizens.

Our old engine houses were in horrible states of disrepair. There were many times when the heat or air conditioning was partially or completely out of service. There were holes in walls and ceilings, as well as unfinished remodeling projects due to a lack of funds. Simple repairs such as a leaky faucet or toilet sometimes took days, or even weeks. We couldn't even purchase garage door remotes and when a door broke, we had to manually open and close it when responding to emergency alarms. This compromised our response time but it didn't seem to matter enough. It got so bad that there were days when we had no toilet paper, paper towels, or dish soap and guys had to get into their own pockets to purchase these items. We had bed bugs, cockroaches, mice, and even raccoons taking up space at our stations. It had become a health issue and was borderline deplorable. A buddy of mine visited our station and described it as similar to a "third-world country" because of its deteriorated condition. He was not too far off!

As they say in the TV show *Shark Tank*, "For these reasons, I am out!" I understood that it was time to go. I needed to bump my retirement date up.

The state auditor said that he saw only two options for the city at this juncture: merging with a neighboring city, or filing Chapter 9 bankruptcy. Merging with the nearby city of Cleveland would be the saving grace for East Cleveland, but it appeared that Cleveland had little or no desire to take on that responsibility because they had very little to gain.

Chapter 9 bankruptcy seemed to me to be the option that the city would have to take. It had happened in Detroit and it was ugly. It was one of those things where it got a lot worse before it got better. This was even more reason for me to retire earlier than I'd planned. If the city did file Chapter 9, then there was a good possibility that I would lose out on my severance pay for unused vacation, compensatory, and sick time. So, with all of these things taken into consideration, I opted to turn in my two-week notice of retirement in late December 2014. My retirement date was now set in stone for January 19, 2015.

I would be 58 years old just a few days after my retirement date and I thought that this was still pretty good, to retire at this age. Most people don't retire until 62 or 65, sometimes later, so I felt fortunate. I also felt good about just making it out safely and in relatively good health. I realized that I would only have a limited number of good years left on this earth and I wanted to try to enjoy them as best I could. I was concerned that my family would have adequate health care and our finances would be sound in retirement. I realized that we would be just fine – not financially worry-free, but comfortable and able to pay the bills, play a lot of golf, and take a few vacations. Retirement felt like the right decision.

It's funny how, in life, things sometimes come full circle. By this I mean that, after a little over twenty-six years, I was now at the end of my career. My son, Michael, had been hired by the Akron Fire Department less than a year before. It was pretty cool for me that as one career ended, another was just beginning. I was so proud of my son for being a firefighter, especially since I never really pressured him into becoming one. The proudest moment in my life as a firefighter was not anything that I did during my career, but instead the day that I was able to pin the badge on my son when he was sworn in to the Akron Fire Department. The timing of the whole thing was truly remarkable and just a beautiful day for our family.

As the days before my retirement passed, I had butterflies in my stomach thinking of my final day with the department. As luck would have it there would be two of us retiring the same day, something that hadn't ever happened before at our small department. My very good Irish-Catholic friend and co-worker, Deputy Chief Tom Flowers, had put his retirement notice in just prior to mine. As fate would have it I had requested, and was granted, a transfer to Tom's shift in

2015. Our last duty day was going to be Sunday, January 18, 2015. Coincidentally this day was also my father's birthday. And, on my last day, my son Michael was permitted to spend the entire day with us as, not just as a guest, but also as a firefighter who would respond with us to emergency runs. What a great way to end a career!

My last day with the department finally came. The trip from Akron to East Cleveland was a bit surreal. It was quite different that day. For starters, my son was riding with me to work for the first time. My mind wandered on the ride there. I thought about some of the guys who had come and gone and the cold hard fact that this was now my turn to move on. As we exited Route 90 onto Eddy Road, I thought of the first time I had driven to East Cleveland more than twenty-six years ago. It was somewhat bittersweet, but the sweet definitely outweighed the bitter. I knew that I was ready to call it quits.

We turned onto Marloes Avenue and parked near fire station number one for the last time. As we entered the building I could sense that the mood was very upbeat. This was a good sign because morale had been low recently due to the uncertainty of our struggling city. The men on duty and some from the oncoming shift were congratulating me immediately. They gathered around us and welcomed my son into their house with open arms. This made me feel very good. They took the edge off for Michael right away. He loved the guys from the start. He remarked later on that the mood was quite different than how it normally is in the morning on shift in Akron. He said it was much livelier and upbeat. It seemed like everybody was in a great mood. It was more like the old days, before the department had taken over the EMS service, when almost every day was upbeat. There was no doubt that we were going to have a great day.

The day, from start to finish, was very relaxed and laid back. After the house work was done in the morning, there would be no more busy work or training going on. The only work that was going to be done was responding to emergencies. Deputy Chief Flowers informed the men on shift that it was "holiday routine," and he and I would not be going on any runs and they would have to handle anything that came up. Realistically I knew that if something serious happened we would respond, but for that day, we would stand down on the not-so-serious calls. I knew my son had stayed up late the night before and I assured him that he could catch a nap right away if he wanted to. I had always been a fan of the "mandatory power nap" and I decided to join Michael in the dormitory for my last nap if he decided to take one. Well, he did, and so did I, but we never did get that nap in because my old buddy, retired firefighter Jeff Polson, came busting through the dormitory door making noise and shouting at me to "get the hell out of that rack!" I knew that there would be no nap for me that day!

I dressed and went downstairs into the kitchen to see Jeff there with a gallon of whiskey, slamming it down from the bottle like it was water. He was in rare form. It was really great to see him. We had fought a lot of fires together over the years and became very close, even though we live about an hour apart and don't get together as often as we should. Jeff was old-school all the way and very rough around the edges, but just a great guy deep down. He was reminiscing and busting everyone's chops, especially the young guys, my son included.

Jeff wasn't the only retiree or former East Cleveland firefighter who stopped in to visit. Russ "Doebuster" Hauser, Chad Johns, Brady "Heat Wave" Howard, Steel Farkas, and Pat Arth also came in to shoot the breeze and break bread with us. It was great to see these guys and talk about the good old days! It's times like this when you realize who your true-blue firefighter friends are. I was a bit surprised when a couple guys who I thought I was close to not only failed to come in on our last day, but also didn't show up the next day at our blowout or the party afterward. Hell, not even a text message congratulation!

Firefighter Tom Buth cooked steaks for everyone, including some of the retired guys who came in to join us. The meal was fantastic, but the camaraderie was even better. It would have been pretty cool if we had one last fire where I could have taken my son inside and shared an adrenaline rush, fighting a good fire. But that didn't happen. We did have a small dryer fire at a laundromat, so I guess I can technically say I responded to an alarm of fire on my last duty day with my son. The rest of the day was fairly uneventful and we slept through most of the night. Shift change is at 8:30 A.M. and on this day, it was also the time of the final "blowout" for Tom and me.

The firefighter on the last night watch has the responsibility of waking the men in the dormitory, as well as the officer in charge, at 7:30 A.M. He is supposed to call the OIC on the telephone and wake the men in the dormitory over the intercom. Firefighter Rich Browne was the watchman on this day. Rich snores so bad that he, as a courtesy to the other firefighters, no longer slept in the dormitory so they could get some rest. He would sleep in the lounge room chairs and take all the night watches, answering the phones and handling the dispatch duties. He decided to spice things up on my last day by playing an old tune over the intercom to wake us up. He shocked everyone out of their sleep by blaring the song "Hit the Road, Jack." It was only fitting and we all got a kick out of it. After the music stopped it hit me that this was it. In one hour I would be walking out of fire station one onto Marloes Avenue for the final blowout!

I dressed and broke down my bedding for the last time. I gathered all of my firefighting turnout gear and stored it in the Fire Prevention Office – all except my helmet, which would be a souvenir for me in my man cave. I was now pretty much ready to get the show on the road.

A little after 8 A.M. I walked toward the kitchen and I could see that a crowd was gathering. You always wonder what kind of a showing you will have at a blowout. It is an indicator of how well you were liked and respected by your co-workers and retirees over the years. It looked like we would have a good number of people there at ours. It didn't hurt that there were two of us leaving (veteran move!).

I walked into the kitchen and was greeted by my good friend Mike Murphy. Mike wasn't a firefighter, but he decided that he was going to drive all the way from Akron to East Cleveland for my blowout. I will always remember this because, due to some personal issues, he hadn't slept in over twenty-four hours. It felt great to have a friend like that, as well as to see the crowd gathering outside. It was also gratifying because it was the middle of January but Mother Nature gave us a break that day with temperatures hovering around 32 degrees.

Tom and I stayed in the kitchen as the clock winded down toward 8:30 A.M. We could hear the fire apparatus pulling out of the engine house and positioning outside onto the apron. The apparatus from station two were also outside, blocking the street as the crowd increased in number. I would guess that there were fifty people or more there and I was pleased that this was a pretty good showing, all things considered. We posed for one last photo with a couple of young ladies who had previously done school-sponsored summer work at fire station one and were well received by the firefighters. They even gave us a nice retirement card. Fire Chief Rick Wilcox snapped the cell phone picture and as he did the sirens started blaring from the five vehicles outside. It was now, after twenty-six years, three months and nine days, time to take the final walk outside of fire station one, and onto a new chapter in life!

As we started outside, arm in arm, the noise was deafening. The sirens and air horns would continue until everyone out there gave us a great big hug and wished their congratulations. So many of my brother firefighters, past and present, were standing there in the middle of the street, clapping, cheering, and shooting cell phone video. The feeling was exhilarating! It is quite an emotional time and guys never know whether they are going to smile, cry, or do both. I wasn't quite sure what I would do.

The crowd made a long semi-circle in the street and others were scattered on the sidewalk and onto the front porch of a neighboring house. I went to the right and Tom to the left and, one by one, we gave everyone out there a hug as words of congratulations and well wishes were exchanged. It was very emotional but the emotion that carried me that day was joy. The tears didn't come. The feeling of elation and a sense of accomplishment and relief were ever-present.

I think the reasons that I didn't cry were two-fold. First of all, the city was in such bad financial condition and the state of the fire department was abysmal, at best. It really was a relief that I was able to retire with good health and a solid pension (state funded, thank God) before the city went belly-up. I did, however, feel for the guys who were not able to retire yet, and had to weather the storm of uncertainty. Secondly, I was extremely excited about starting a house-flipping business with my son. We had been talking about it for a few years and, since I was now able to access my retirement savings, it would be possible.

I thought about being retired and the best thing about it, to me, was the ability to control my own time. If you think about it, your time is controlled from the moment you are born until the day you retire. You are mandated to be at school when you are younger. Then, for most of your adult life, you are mandated to be at work. You are told what to do by teachers in school, then by bosses at work. When you retire you have the ability to make your own schedule, go at your own pace, and answer to no bosses for the first time in your life. It took me fifty-eight years to get to that point and the feeling was liberating!

After all of the hugs and well wishes were given we took a few group photos, then about twenty-five of us went to breakfast – at a place that served alcohol. Yes indeed, it was time for a celebration. Firefighters happen to be very skilled at drinking and celebrating life. The normal routine for a post-blowout celebration is breakfast then onto downtown Cleveland for the "bar crawl." This day would be no different. As a veteran of these events I know that as time goes by during the day, people will come and go, and you typically end up with five or six hardcore partiers at the end of the night in a bar, shit-faced drunk, with beer goggles on, telling war stories, and professing our love for each other! I happened to absolutely love nights like this and have been a part of at least a few in my career. Since this was my blowout, there was no way I could even consider shutting it down early, even though I was fifty-seven years old. The same went for Tom. He would be there until the end. My son Michael paid for a hotel room at the Renaissance Hotel in downtown Cleveland to avoid the DUI gauntlet of driving back to Akron under the influence. It was truly a wise decision!

Well, we did the marathon and hit it hard until the wee hours. I appreciated the effort put forth by some of the last men standing, Dan Vicarel, Chad Johns, Richard Gist, Joe Mucic, and Steel Farkas. We went to a number of bars, and a few gentlemen's clubs through the course of the day – and night. Everybody had a great time, spent way too much money, and got home safe, just as we do in the fire service. We go home safe. At least that is our number-one priority! Nobody got into a fight or was arrested. We talked about all the good times because there were so many. We slobbered all over each other with beer goggles on. We held each other up at the end of the night and made sure that nobody got hurt. I assured the younger firefighters that things will get better in East Cleveland and that they will be okay. I hoped and prayed that things would work out for them because those firefighters are what I will always miss most about the job. Not the job itself, even though I loved it, but the guys! It's always about the guys! My brothers!

Firefighter, soon to be Lieutenant, Richard Gist gave me a ride back to the Renaissance Hotel. We had spent a lot of time on shift together toward the end of my career and I really became close to him. I was glad that Richard, a black man, was there until the end with us. I didn't want it to be just the white guys because our department was so diverse. That meant a lot to me because we, like many of the black and white firefighters and officers, were brothers for life! I was happy that both races were there until the end of the night.

As I walked into the Renaissance, I thought that this day couldn't have been better. I realized that my career in East Cleveland had been a life-altering, phenomenal experience. That day, just like my career, was now officially over. It was time to go to bed, but my son wasn't with me. Hopefully he was already in our hotel room. I stumbled my way through the lobby and into the elevator. I was feeling no pain and was in a great state of mind. I just wanted to go back to the room and see my son in there so I could fall asleep with no worries. It was now about 2:30 A.M. and I was pretty sure that Michael was already in the room. I walked into the room and, to my surprise, he was not there. I knew that he wasn't alone when I last saw him and that the guys would make sure he was okay before everyone left. So, I hit the bed and was fast asleep, probably in less than a minute.

I woke up early in the morning to go to the bathroom and, sure enough, there was Michael in the bed next to mine, sound asleep, snoring like a Grizzly. This was the icing on the cake and now I was completely content, knowing that he was okay. I didn't know how he got there and I didn't really care. I was just glad that he was safe. Things had truly come full circle and I couldn't have been happier and prouder to be there with my only son. After twenty-six years with the East Cleveland Fire Department, I could still claim that "Everyone got home safe!"

"Everyone got home safe!"

–Michael C. Ede

www.ingramcontent.com/pod-product-compliance
Lightning Source LLC
Chambersburg PA
CBHW050633160426
43194CB00010B/1657